ABSOLUTELY
SIXTEEN FEET

— Deviation From The Divine Game Plan
Will Produce Disaster —

Philemon G. Roberts, MDiv, DMin

CLERGY COLLECTIONS
PRESERVING THE BEST
FOR THE NEXT GENERATION

A sub-division of Post-Gutenberg Books

ABSOLUTELY SIXTEEN FEET

Copyright © 2013 by Philemon G. Roberts

Library of Congress Control Number: 2013939083

Roberts, Philemon G. 1932 -

ABSOLUTELY SIXTEEN FEET: Deviation From the Divine Game
Plan Will Produce Disaster

ISBN 978-1-935434-19-1

Subject Codes and Description: 1: REL012000: Religion: Christian
Life - General 2: REL012040: Religion: Christian Life - Inspirational 3:
REL006980: Religion: Christian Life.

Cover Design by Barton Green

Printed in Australia, France, Germany, Italy, Spain, UK, and USA

Published by

CLERGY COLLECTIONS

a subdivision of Post Gutenberg Books
an imprint of GlobalEdAdvance Press

It is with great pleasure that I dedicate this book
to my bride of over sixty years

Betty V. Roberts

Whatever success and accomplishments I have achieved,
I owe to her. She has always supported me: whether it
be in the pastorate, in my educational pursuits, or in any
attempt to give service to the Kingdom. She was, and is,
God's gift to me.

"More people are humbugged into believing too little, rather than too much."

P.T. Barnum is reported to have said this quote. It was probably a defensive statement, inasmuch as Barnum was much criticized and maligned for the theatrical trickery and gimmickry that allowed him to acquire great wealth because of the gullibility of the masses. However, he was probably correct!

Contents

I personally deplore the closed-minded retreat into little groups where one fails to receive any spark of challenge to one's ideas concerning Biblical interpretation. Unless one's doctrinal views are subjected to the red-hot crucible of give-and-take and can stand the challenge of someone else's opinions, those doctrinal views are, at least, suspect. After all, the Bible says, "Iron sharpens iron," and doctrinal views that cannot withstand the challenge of one's enemies (as well as friends) leave something to be desired.

Preface

The following twelve sermons by Philemon G. Roberts, are part of Clergy Collections, preserving the best of the past for the next generation. Read them carefully; Dr. Roberts speaks based on authoritative Scripture where God is clear and means what He says. It is true that some do not clearly understand the translated scripture and the word usage, but that does not change the original intent.

A clear understanding of sacred writings comes through the illumination of the Holy Spirit and diligent study by the preacher. The effort is to understand the meaning of words in the original language and how best to express them to the current culture.

————————

Publisher's note: The archaic language of the King James Bible references are preserved to maintain the time frame and true nature of the religious discourse presented in this book.

"To live up above, with the saints we love,
Oh, that will be glory!
But to live here below, with the saints we know,
Well, that's another story!"

1

Absolutely Sixteen Feet

Iwas traveling on a summer vacation and observed an astonishing sign. Just before the vehicle dipped underneath an overpass, a road sign read "Absolutely Sixteen Feet." My inquisitive nature got the best of me and I conjectured why such a sign was needed. I unearthed, in my mental cogitations, several likely reasons for this distinctive sign. First, I assumed some rather large truck had struck the overpass. The poor driver had protested to the authorities that one knows that there is always a few inches to spare; we never speak absolutely about anything. Another fellow protested, after crunching the top of his big rig, that everyone knows that men always speak figuratively – nothing in this world is absolute. Finally, an exasperated road department official penned this eye-catching sign: "Absolutely Sixteen Feet" – no more, no less.

God has always dealt with man in such a manner. Deuteronomy 11:26-28 says, "Behold, I set before you this day a blessing, and a curse; A blessing if ye obey the commandments of the Lord your God, which I Command you this day: And a curse, if ye will not obey the commandments of the Lord your God, but turn aside out of the way which I command you this day." God makes rules; men must play by His rules. Any deviation from God's game plan will produce disaster. This day of situation ethics, moral permissiveness, conditional promises and the like, is not in conformity with God's plan. The demands of God are absolute, irrevocable, and precise; any deviation from them will bring disastrous results.

God made planet earth for a purpose. Isaiah 45:18 said that "... God himself that formed the earth and made it... he formed it to be inhabited." When planet earth was formed, it was designed to be a great research center to test man. For instance, when a great industrial complex develops a new product (before such an item is deemed marketable and worthy of production), it must undergo exhaustive tests to prove its worth. These tests will reveal its defects and shortcomings. In a similar manner, man had to prove himself worthy of the things that God had planned for him. He had to fulfill a probationary state before he could be raised from "glory to glory" (II Corinthians 3:18). Thus the original intention of God was not thwarted; out of the chaotic mess, God brought forth new forms of animal life, fish and fowl. Out of the rubble of the original creation, God formed and fashioned a new earth.

On the sixth day of this re-creation, God created His crowning achievement – man. Genesis 5:1, 2 says, "In the day that God created man, in the likeness of God made he him; Male and female created he them; and blessed them, and called their name Adam, in the day when there were created." Can you imagine the feeling of Satan? Here was a rival; here was an object to be tested and tried. After all, the fall of Lucifer had converted him into the "tempter." His nature had now degenerated into that of one who would tempt, who would destroy. Thus we must be on guard: "Be sober, be vigilant; because your adversary the devil, as a roaring lion, walketh about, seeking whom he may devour;

Whom resist steadfast in the faith, knowing that the same afflictions are accomplished in your brethren that are in the world" (I Peter 5:8, 9).

The new couple received some instructions. Listen to Genesis 1:28: "Be fruitful, and multiply, and replenish the earth, and subdue it: and have dominion over the fish of the sea, and over the fowl of the air, and over every living thing that moveth upon the earth." Also, let us note the words of Genesis 1:26: "... and let them have dominion. ..." Thus Adam and Eve were given certain privileges and rights over the earth.

But remember this, God had placed in rulership over the earth (Ezekiel 28:14-16: Luke 4:6) that angel known as Lucifer. And now, in a sense, God had placed one in Satan's territory, and had given this new creation, man, rights and authorities over this planet earth. Can you imagine the thoughts of Satan? What does God think He is doing? What does He mean by placing one, made lower than the angels, over this earth? The devil's pride must have come forth in full regalia. "Look at me, made higher than all angelic creatures – whether they be seraphs, cherubim's, or what have you. And look at that puny creature called man, who has been designated as my replacement over this world." One can imagine that Satan licked his chops with relish as he viewed this new challenge.

But let us relish a few hors d'eouvres at this point (we will expand these points in later chapters). Proverbs 16:18 says, "Pride goeth before destruction, and an haughty spirit before a fall." Satan had said "I will" five times in the book of Isaiah when he had conceived in his heart a naughty suggestion of evil; but one day God is going to put the "I's, " out; and the "kingdoms of this world are becoming the kingdoms of our Lord, and of his Christ; and he shall reign forever and ever" (Revelations 11:15). God, much like a good chess player, will sometimes use the strategy of a "gambit" – he will sacrifice (to appearances) in an initial move in order to gain a final victory.

Before we deal with the attempt of Satan to usurp the kingdom and dominion that God had placed in man's hand, let us first look at this creation called "man." Before we can understand how Satan tempted man, and even how man can be attacked by evil spirits today, we must first of all understand something about this new creation – man. Genesis 1:26 and 27 says that God made man in "His own image." Yes, man is made in the image of God. I do not intend to get into a full-fledged theological debate about the image of God in man. However, a few Scriptural facts will let us know the basic facts about the image of God in man, and what it really is.

We know that God is a Trinity, and man is, in a real sense, a tripartite or three-part creature. I Thessalonians 5:23 says, "I pray God your whole spirit and soul and body be preserved blameless." Man, then, in his essential being is spirit, soul and body. Let us look at them in reverse order. The "body" is the material part of man by which he has "world consciousness." The "soul" is the part of man that feels – by it he has affections, emotions and passions, and thus he has "self-consciousness." The highest part of man is the "spirit" of man. This part of man knows and wills things. This attribute lifts man above the brute beast of the field, and makes him a free-moral agent. Animals have bodies and souls, but not a spirit. And the most important thing about this spirit part of man is that it gives him "God-consciousness." (Note: A careful Scriptural study of these elements will reveal a definite blurring of the descriptive elements of soul and spirit.)

Now where, precisely, does the image of God fit into this structure of man? The Bible declares that "God is a spirit." Jesus declared that a spirit is "not flesh and bones" (Luke 24:39). Now do not misunderstand this statement. Some Bible scholars emphasize God's spirit being so excessively that He has no form, no substance at all. I cannot believe that. But God's form is spirit (whatever that essence is), and it is not composed of flesh and bones. There it is: that part of man which was made in the image of God was and is spiritual in nature.

Then Ephesians 4:23, 24 tells us that man should be "renewed in the spirit of his mind" and that he should "put on the new man which after God is created in righteousness and true holiness." And in Colossians 3:10 we are told to "put on the new man, which is renewed in the knowledge after the image of Him that created him." Thus the moral features of the original image were: Knowledge, righteousness and holiness (of truth).

Friend, the reason God placed man on earth was to have someone on earth to manifest the glory of God in a visible fashion. God did not send His Son to Calvary primarily to save man from hell; rather, he redeemed man so that he could fulfill the functions for which he was first created – communion with God and a reflection of the glory of God. This is what God wants, even today, on this earth. Hear the Word: "Blessed are the pure in heart: for they shall see God" (Matthew 5:8), and "Be ye therefore perfect, even as your Father which is in heaven is perfect" (Matthew 5:48). And, "That He might present it to himself a glorious church, not having spot, or wrinkle, or any such thing; but that it should be holy and without blemish" (Ephesians 5:27). And in I Peter 1:16: "... Be ye holy; for I am holy." God placed man here to reflect the glory of God through the divine image of God within man's being.

I believe we can see what Satan had to achieve; and what he has to achieve today. As long as the spirit portion of man functioned as it was created, man could commune with God; he could obey God; his life was God-centered and God-controlled. But when man surrendered his will to Satan, Satan gained the ascendancy in his life, Satan gained control. Thus when man fell, man's spirit, which was intended to be the dwelling place of God, became the domain and abode of Satan and all manner of evil spirits. Thus man became "dead in trespasses and sins" (Ephesians 2:1). Oh, not dead in body, not physically dead – but separated from God, so that for all intents and purposes man is dead to the things of God. Man's spirit is thus dead in trespasses and sins, and he cannot find God until his spirit is "quickened" (made alive – Ephesians 2:5). When the breath of God blows anew on man, he will have his deadened spirit regenerated, and he will begin to again have fellowship with His maker.

These facts lead us to a sobering (but often overlooked) fact: the battle that you and I face is a spiritual battle. We imagine that our battles are those things out there – we see our enemies and number them; we think that if communism could be destroyed, the world's political systems would be all right. No! The real battle is not out there where we can visibly observe it. Ephesians 6:12 makes this plain: "For we wrestle not against flesh and blood, but against principalities, against powers, against the rulers of the darkness of this world, against spiritual wickedness in

high places." The battlefield is locatable – it is not in the
realm of the visible, but the invisible. The Scripture says,
"Let this mind be in you, which was also in Christ Jesus"
(Philippians 2:5), and "...be renewed in the spirit of your
mind" (Ephesians 4:23). There is where Adam and Eve were
attacked; and this is where we will also be attacked. Was
not the prophet's servant surprised when God opened his
eyes and he saw an innumerable host of creatures around
Dothan (II Kings 6:17)? Our flesh makes us so earthly-
oriented and earthly-confined that we fail to recognize the
true source of conflict.

Thus God made man and his helpmate, woman, and
placed them in the Garden of Eden. Here were the new
king and queen of planet earth. Man has never since found
himself in such favorable and propitious circumstances.
They were the rulers; commissioned by the Almighty to
"subdue" it and to have "dominion" over it. It was theirs to
do with as they willed. But into that Paradise strolled Satan.

Wherever there is good, the devil is seeking to destroy
it. Let a church become a lighthouse for the lost and
the devil will intrude. Let a man and woman dedicate
themselves to consistent, total Christian living, and the
enemy of our souls will attack with vengeance. You seek
to declare the glory and power of God above the Devil, and
you will have the greatest battle of your life. Attend church,
enter into a rhapsodic experience with the Almighty, declare
your intent to tread upon the powers of evil, and the devil
will await behind a bush outside the sanctuary to hound you
and nip your heels the full of the coming week.

I never tire of a true to life illustration I heard on one
occasion. A slave owner had invited a rather religious black
man to go duck hunting with him. On their way to the duck

pond, the slave owner chided his slave about his religion. "Why, Sam, you pretend to be religious, but you are always having trouble. The devil is always after you. But look at me – I am prosperous, successful. I have everything I want. Can you explain that, Sam?"

The man replied rather soulfully, "Now boss man, you won't get mad at me if I tells you the truth will you?"

"Of course not," replied the boss.

"It's like this, Massa'. You and I are going duck hunting. Now if we should see a flock of ducks flying over, you will fire into those ducks. Now suppose one of them falls dead at your feet, and the others begin to scamper away. Which one of those ducks will you chase, Massa'?"

"Why," retorted the master, "That's a foolish question, Sam. You know I would chase the wounded duck. I already have in my possession the dead one."

"That's what I'm trying to tell you, Massa'. The devil knows you is a dead duck. That's the reason he leaves you alone."

So the devil attacks this godly pair who had pristine holiness in their beings. First, the devil planted a doubt in the woman's mind when he said, "Yea, hath God said, Ye shall not eat of every tree of the garden?" (Genesis 3:1). If man can be made to doubt God, to doubt the veracity of the Scriptures, the evil one is halfway to victory. How many are snared by that kind of thinking. Does God really mean it when He says that He will allow people to go to hell? Is He not a God of love, and are not judgment and damnation incompatible with such a nature? Does God mean it when He says that he will judge sins? Surely not every little sin? And so today, men fill pulpits who do not believe in the Word of God: they find the Genesis cosmogony (truth about the universe's origination) to be mythical and archaic. They hold no sure standard of righteousness and sin is neither black nor white, but a shaded grey. And the world is being led down a dead-end street as the "blind lead the blind" and "both... fall into the ditch" (Matthew 15:14).

"All right," said Satan, "what did God really say?" Eve replied, "We may eat of the fruit of the trees in the garden: but of the fruit of the tree which is in the midst of the garden, God hath said, Ye shall not eat of it, neither shall ye touch it, lest ye die" (Genesis 3:2, 3). Eve made the second fatal mistake, she began to add to the Scripture (Revelation 22:19). She said, "... or touch it." She was making sin something tangible, something you touch. Sin is not in things, it is in the mind. It is a state of the soul.

Then Satan moved in; he had the woman on the rocks. These words spoke Satan to the wavering woman, "Ye shall not surely die" (Genesis 3:4). When Satan gets you to believing that sin is OK, then he is ready to give you a K.O. "Look Eve," said the serpent, "God is holding out on you. Eat from this beautiful tree and you'll move up where God is." Eve succumbed to the devil's logic, and that beautiful, holy creature, Eve, who was clothed with a beautiful light from God, became a naked, godless creature. It took some talking to convince Eve, but Adam gave in without a fight. "And it was not Adam who deceived, but the woman being quite deceived fell into transgression." (I Timothy 2:14).

And man has been plucking fruit from the forbidden tree ever since, despite the fact that God has said, "Love not the world, neither the things that are in the world. If any man love the world, the love of the Father is not in him. For all that is in the world (or characterizes this world-system), the lust of the flesh, and the lust of the eyes, and the pride of life (good for food, pleasant to the eye, to be desired to make one wise) is not of the Father, but is of the world" (I John 2:15-17). But cheer up, friend, the battle is far from lost. The apostle John, however, states that "... the world passeth away, and the lust thereof; but he that doeth the will of God abideth forever." It is true that the transformed man lives in a hostile environment; beset on every hand by evil forces. But while the earthly, worldly-minded man puts his stakes in a system that shall deteriorate and fall and decay; God's regenerated man belongs to a system of an incorruptible nature. God has thankfully, planted a little substation, a branch office of heaven on this earth. And its constituents look forward to the day when the will of God will be "done in earth as it is in heaven" (Matthew 6:10).

Man failed to play by God's rules; he violated God's absolute commands and, in the light of the Scripture we have surveyed, we must admit that the rulership of this world passed from Adam and Eve into the hands of the Devil in the Garden of Eden. Contrary to what some might think, the legal property rights to this world-system is in the hands of Satan. In Luke the fourth chapter, Satan took Jesus up into a high place, and there he showed Him all the kingdoms of the world in a moment of time. And Satan challenged my Lord by saying, "For that (the whole earth and the glory of its kingdoms) has been delivered unto me!" And my Lord, not one time, challenged Satan's right to make this statement. Three times Christ Himself referred to Satan as the "prince of this world" (John 12:31; 14:30; 16:11). Paul said that Satan is "god of this world" (II Corinthians 4:4). John, the apostle, said that "... the whole world lieth in wickedness" (I John 5:19). Yes, my friend, Adam and Eve handed over the deed of trust to this world to Satan, and transferred their allegiance from the "Father of lights" to the "father of lies." And today, man has a similar choice. Romans 6:16 says, "Know ye not, that to whom ye yield yourselves servants to obey, his servants ye are to whom ye obey; whether of sin unto death, or of obedience unto righteousness?"

But I thank God the final chapter has not been written; the final song has not been sung; the final act has not been staged. Satan may have won a battle in the Garden; but he has not won the war. When Satan came to Jesus in Luke he attempted to have Jesus trade the whole universe (which was under the feet of the Son, the last Adam, Psalm 8:6) to him by a momentary act of worship. But Jesus defeated Satan when He said, "Get thee hence, Satan!" (Matthew 4:10) Christ was a "Son over His own house" (Hebrews 3:6); that is, over the redeemed ones. He came to redeem this world lying in death, by his own death, so "that through death he might destroy him that had the power of death, that is, the devil" (Hebrews 2:14). Those words have filtered into our theology and doctrine, redemption, salvation, purchasing, etc., all acknowledge that the control of planet earth had to be wrested, through some moral means, from the grasp of Satan.

Although God, for moral reasons, recognized the passing of control of the earth's sphere from Adam and Eve to Satan, yet Almighty God retains sovereignty in this universe. And the children of His kingdom, even today, are not subject to the kingdom of darkness. He "hath raised us up together, and made us sit together in heavenly places in Christ Jesus. That in the ages to come he might shew the exceeding riches of his grace..." (Ephesians 2:6, 7). One day, by God's grace, we shall join in that heavenly choir and sing,

"The kingdoms of this world are becoming the kingdoms of our Lord, and of His Christ, and He shall reign forever and ever... We give thee thanks, O Lord God Almighty... because thou hast taken to thee thy great power, and hast reigned!" (Revelation 11:15, 17).

2

The Devil Made Me Do It

How many people have laughed themselves silly at the wild antics of the inimitable comedian Flip Wilson. Sashaying on to the television screen with a demure, coy walk, he voices the apologetic words of Geraldine: "The devil made me do it... why, the devil made me buy this new dress." And we all join in uncontrollable laughter at this realistic portrayal of human nature.

But his satanic majesty is no laughing matter. C. S. Lewis, in his *Screwtape Letters*, vividly depicts one of the demonic characters from the nether world as he deploys his sinister stratagems against us feeble worldlings. And, contrary to what one might suppose, his devious plan does not entail outright rejection of belief in God or the Devil. Rather, he promotes faith – only let it be faith that is weak and void of real belief. He even promotes church attendance – only let it be a casual, pretentious attendance at the house of God.

For years men have dismissed the devil (he is a character made possible by the superstitious beliefs of the ignorant) – but today we have more devil than we have ever had. Anton Lavey and his *Satanic Bible* is but one of a number of devices that are promoting his Satanic highness. Old Lucifer seems to be brewing a cauldron of witches brew today that has spilled over into this world with fury. For years men denied him, but now the pendulum has swung to the other extreme – they have begun to worship him. Like a slimy reptilian creature, Satan has slithered out from under a rock and has shown himself as the powerful, mystifying creature he really is.

What has brought this world to the place that it is today? A daily reading of the morning newspaper is nothing more no less than a stroll through the morgue and a crawl through the gutter. Lurid tales of evil await the reader; unconscionable acts of terror and unrighteousness abound. The only sobering element in the whole endeavor is an occasional piece of good sandwiched between the evil.

Yes, fortunately, there is good as well as evil in the universe. There is a degree of peace and tranquility that helps to preserve one's sanity, and keeps the mind from shattering into a million pieces. But the man of reason begins to question, "If God is good why does He allow all this evil? Why does He not abolish the devil if there is one?" All these questions tend to dovetail into a greater question: "Where did all this begin anyway?"

Let us go back to the beginning – not the beginning of God, because God had no beginning ("For I am the Lord, I change not" – Malachi 3:6). But, rather, let us return to the beginning of the earth, of man, of the various creatures who have roamed this planet earth since its conception. Somewhere in that prehistoric era there was a moment when time was squeezed out of eternity. It may be illustrated by a bead of water forming on the side of a glass; one moment it didn't exist, and the next moment it appeared, fully formed and observable by the human eye.

In the first two chapters of the Bible we have the so-called "Creation account." God has, momentarily, drawn back the veil of the past and has given us a glimpse of the sole record of earth's first stages. "In the beginning God created the heaven and the earth" (Gen. 1:1). And then suddenly, without further explanation, the mood and tone of Scripture takes a sudden twist: "And the earth was without form and void; and darkness was upon the face of the deep. And the Spirit of God moved upon the face of the waters" (Gen. 2:1). Verse two paints a picture of a chaotic condition of the earth. Did God create a cosmos (world; order) that was chaos (dis-order)? The question almost answers itself since the word chaos means "total disorder or confusion." I think the answer to that question must bring an emphatic "No!"

Listen to Isaiah 45:18: "For thus saith the Lord that created the heavens; God himself that formed the earth and made it; he created it not in vain, he formed it to be inhabited: I am the Lord; and there is none else." This Scripture says that He created it not "without form and void" – the condition we find it in verse two of Genesis one.

If we were talking about man, we would all agree that anything that he touches will bear the imprint of his imperfectness. Not so with God. It is simply not the nature of God to create sinful or imperfect things. James says, "Doth a fountain send forth at the same place sweet water and bitter? ...so can no fountain both yield salt water and fresh" (James 3:11, 12). Can a God who is perfectly good do evil? Can a God who is perfect in all His ways create imperfection? The answer is rather obvious. Palms 18:30 says, "As for God, his way is perfect. ..." Jesus Himself said that "A good man out of the good treasure of the heart bringeth forth good things: and an evil man out of the evil treasure bringeth forth evil things" (Matthew 12:35).

It is a rather low, inconceivably poor view of God that would impute to Him evil; that could believe that the Creator would begin with Chaos. Who could even imagine that good could give birth to evil. Admittedly man takes the good and perverts it into the bad. Man can take purity and besmirch and contaminate it until it is only a vestige of its former self. But not God; He begins with that which is pure and holy, passes it on to men, and must, with longsuffering and patience, watch men pervert it. No! We must believe that a perfect God created a good and perfect earth.

If God created a perfect earth in Genesis 1:1, what took place that perverted this marvelous earth of verse one? We believe that the Bible gives a hint as to this reason. Something catastrophic must have taken place between these two verses. Something of more than casual significance must have produced this great abyss, this yawning gap. We use these terms "abyss" and "gap" with good reason. It is at this point that we believe there was the spawning, as far as this earth was concerned, of a consummate wickedness that injected an awful evil into this universe.

But let us go back farther, even farther than the day of Genesis 1:1. Yes, even before the beginning of the earth, God created certain beings called angels. The word "angel" actually means "messenger." The word angel can sometimes refer to a human being who is God's fleshly messenger. But these beings of whom we speak are "spirit beings"; they were created sometime before the beginning of the planet earth. That perfect and upright man Job poses this profound question: "Where wast thou when I laid the foundations of the earth...?" (Job 38:4). He goes on to tell us that there were creatures other than God present when the earth was created. He continues with this question: "Where wast thou, ...When the morning stars sang together, and all the sons of God shouted for joy?" (Job 38:7). I find no figurative language here; I see a veritable host of angelic creatures singing ecstatic songs of joy and praise. And what blessed harmony must have prevailed at this particular songfest; for **all** the sons of God joined in that singing at the morn of creation. Unquestionably, there were angelic creatures in this universe even before the creation of the earth.

Now, who were these spirit beings? These angels? We might interject at this point the fact that many theologians believe the angels were created one at a time; thus their number is neither larger no smaller than at the original time of creation (Matthew 22:28-30). We have no specific, detailed account of their creation; however, Paul does give us an insight into this matter in Colossians 1:16: "For by him (Christ) were all things created, that are in heaven, and that are in earth, visible and invisible, whether they be thrones, or dominions, or principalities, or powers: all things were created by him and for him." We must observe that these "principalities" and "powers" are angels or spheres of angelic operation.

Did these creatures play a part in the murky interval in the first chapter of Genesis? We believe they did; we believe they played a prominent role in this chaos of the cosmos. One of the lead angels, possibly one of at least two archangels, appears to be the cunning culprit who instigated this sordid event. Ezekiel 28 gives us an insight into an event that involves this prime suspect. In an illustration of the law of "double reference," Ezekiel makes reference to an individual beyond the earthly king of Tyrus (28:12). This creature was created perfect and walked up and down in the mineral garden of Eden (we believe this should be differentiated from the Garden of Genesis 3). He was a beautiful creature; his mind was sharp and wise.

Isaiah, the 14th chapter, gives us further insight into Lucifer (Satan) and the cause of his fall. This beautiful creature, vested with every grace and anointed as the guardian of God's glory – this creature said, "I will ascend into heaven, I will exalt my throne above the stars of God: I will sit also upon the mount of the congregation, in the sides of the north: I will ascend above the heights of the clouds; I will be like the most High" (Isa. 14:13, 14). What was his sin? Pride! I Timothy 3:6 makes this clear when it says, "... lest being lifted up with pride he fall into the condemnation of the devil." "I... I... I..." An egomania seized this bright cherub and caused his self-exaltation. No one can ever be humble until the "I's" have been put out.

How could Satan fall? It is true that the angelic creatures were endowed with superhuman powers. Peter pointed out that angels "are greater in power and might" than are men (II Peter 2:11). Men, in fact, according to Hebrews 2:7, are made a little "lower than the angels." (Worthy of note is the fact that Christ is made "so much better than the angels Hebrews 1:4). But God also endowed angels with free wills. A creature is never more than a "thing" unless he has a free will. Robots and automatons respond with programmed responses; but free-will creatures respond with inner impulses based upon a freedom of choice. The love and praise that God hears from men and angels is not elicited by force or electronic programming. It must be freely given.

Sadness grips our hearts when we think about those creatures who sacrificed such great opportunities and marvelously good conditions for a momentary lark or thrill. The greater heights from which one falls, the greater, humanly speaking, the fall. The most astounding fall this universe has ever witnessed was the fall of Lucifer. Think about it! This creature had his habitation in heaven. His dwelling place was the third heaven. Heaven – where "the angels do always behold the face of my Father" (Matthew 18:10). He was a member of that beloved group "... the angels of heaven" (Matthew 24:36). He was in that place from which "Jesus shall be revealed (from heaven) with his mighty angels" (II Thessalonians 1:7). It was here that Satan lifted up his heart in rebellion against God. Thus Jesus Christ refers back to those eons past when He saw "Satan as lightning fall from heaven" (Luke 10:18). That untimely rebellion cost Satan his job and brought about his banishment from the kingdom of God.

But the sadness of this situation, as with so many others, was not that Satan alone fell; but that a large number of others bore the consequences of his prideful, willful rebellion against Creator God. As with all sinners, the consequences of their sinning extends to others. Numberless others are affected by the slightest ripple on the tranquil sea of time. When Satan fell he carried myriad others of the angelic host with him; henceforth, they shall be known as "fallen angels" or "demons." Thankfully, a host of "ministering spirits" or "angels of God" (Hebrews 1:14) did not yield to the pride of Satan (Hebrews 12:22; Revelation 5:11). But we know that vast numbers of these fallen angels or demons prowl the earth, and the devil himself "as a roaring lion, walketh about, seeking whom he may devour" (I Peter 5:8).

Some men claim they do not believe in the devil. How can one explain the sin that is prevalent in the earth? How does one explain the newsworthy events that display evil so blatant and rotten that the mind of a sane, sensible person cannot even fathom the motivation or reason for such rottenness. Listen to this sickening confession: "He (Houston) lay there, and Bill told him and said, 'Smile, Satan; smile'; and He (Houston) smiled, just kind of a sickly grin, at which time all I could think of to do was spit in his mouth, so I did several times." This nauseous verbiage was the confession of a murderer in the so-called "Satanic trial" recently held in a southern city. Like a slimy mass, sin moves across this earth; fomented by the mastermind of evil: The Devil.

My friend, we are dealing with the devil and his henchmen. This demonic spirit is no novice. He who once had wisdom above his fellows in his first estate in heaven, has become perverted. Now he uses the same wisdom to carry out his evil designs. The fantastic genius that he used to help rule for Almighty God, has been twisted and perverted into a devilish usage by which he rules the heart of unregenerate men. He once knew holiness and righteousness as it was delivered from the hand of God Himself; but now he has fallen into the lowest depths of sin and evil. He has run with the hare and hunted with the hounds; he has lived on both sides of the tracks. He knows how to play any game man can devise, and he knows how to play it well. For thousands of years, for many millenniums, he has devised schemes to grip and trap every son of the living God. His dexterity and skill, his adroitness and consummate wisdom have not vanished. He knows how to dangle delightful tidbits before men; he knows how to ensnare and trap them. "Watch out, the devil will get you if you don't watch out" is more than a catchy phrase.

For all intents and purposes, then, the beginning of the Devil was the beginning of evil. Somebody has pleaded, "Why does not God kill the devil?" A portion of the answer can be posited by asking another question: "Why does not God kill us – you and me?" The devil, unfortunately, is not the only sinner. Obviously, God would have to destroy the preponderant portion of the human race before evil could be banished from this earth. And we suppose that Noah and the seven others saved with him, bespeak of the futility of even saving a few.

But God has chosen to allow the devil to roam the earth. Among other titles, we known that Satan is the "Tempter" (Matthew 4:3, I Thessalonians 3:5). His cunning wiles are allowed because mortal man is on a probationary sojourn; man must be tested and proven. In the same manner that the diamond is subjected to the tools and devices of the stone artisan, you and I are proven faithful when we reject the inferior wares of the devil. Man must prove himself worthy of God's blessings. In order for this to be done, there must be a form of temptation. The devil and his angels provide this temptation.

When we see the wars and rumors of wars; when we see the pestilence and strife that pervade this land we cry, "Lord, why, why, Lord?" An old hymn asks the same question:

> *"Tempted and tried, we're oft made to wonder,*
> *Why it should be thus all the day long,*

While there are others living about us,
Never molested tho' in the wrong.
(Chorus)
Farther along we'll know all about it, Farther along,
We'll understand why;
Cheer up, my brother, live in the sunshine,
We'll understand it all by and by."

When Jesus was approached by the Devil, Matthew says "the tempter" came to Jesus (Matthew 4:3). Paul, writing to the church at Thessalonica, uses the same term: "For verily, when we were with you, we told you before that we should suffer tribulation; even as it came to pass, and ye know. For this cause, when I could no longer forbear, I sent to know your faith, lest by some means the **tempter** have tempted you, and our labour be in vain" (I Thessalonians 3:4, 5). Later on in II Thessalonians (1:5), we are told that our persecutions and tribulations come in order to show that we endure and "may be counted worthy of the kingdom of God."

Nonetheless, until the glorious day of divine deliverance, we must not underestimate our enemy. Many armies have crumbled before the onslaught of the enemy when they underestimated his resources. Fortunately, the Scriptures do not underestimate our foe. We are taught that the course of this world and age is directed by the prince of the power of the air – Satan (Ephesians 2:2). This is even further confirmed by the fact that the whole world lies in the wicked one (I John 5:19), and that Satan is even the "god of this world" (II Corinthians 4:4). A further insight into the power of this demonic spirit is revealed when we are told in the book of Jude that when Michael, an archangel (a member of the highest order of angelic beings), disputed with the devil about the body of Moses he "durst (dared) not bring against him a railing accusation" (vs. 9). So powerful was this foe of Michael, the Devil, that Michael had to appeal to the Lord for assistance.

Yes, my friend, this angelic "star," Satan, who dragged one-third of the heavenly hosts down with him in his fall (Revelation 12:4), is still attempting to drag men and women down to damnation. He has been, and is, unrelenting in his task. He has an inexorable purpose and he is pursuing it with merciless means. It is the devil who is causing all the trouble in the world, and we need to know his devices. James 1:13 says that "God cannot be tempted with evil, neither tempteth he any man." The tempter is the devil, or Satan (Matthew 4:3). Next to God himself he is the most powerful force in this universe, therefore, we must beware.

We must expect opposition from the devil. There are certain laws of nature that can only operate effectively when there is opposition, yet they produce beneficial results – gravity, inertia, etc. Thus it can be with the Devil. One man made a statement to the effect that he expected to run into the devil every morning. One fellow, who was quite curious, asked "Why?" The man responded: "Because if I do not have a collision with him every day, I would be concerned lest he and I should be going in the same direction."

Why deal with the devil? Why spend time talking about one who seeks our destruction? The answer is obvious. If one is fighting an enemy he needs to know everything possible about that enemy – his strengths, his weaknesses, his devices, his plan of procedure. Our Bible says that we must "Be sober, be vigilant; because your adversary the devil, as a roaring lion, walketh about, seeking whom he may devour: Whom resist steadfast in the faith" (I Peter

5:8, 9). James writes, "Submit yourselves therefore to God. *Resist* the devil and he will flee from you" (4:7). And a mighty challenge is given in II Corinthians 2:9, 11: "For to this end did I write, that I might know the proof of you, whether ye be obedient in all things. ... Lest Satan should get an advantage of us: for we are not ignorant of his devices." Need we say more?

However, we would be derelict in our duty if we emphasized our "enemy" to the exclusion of our "ally." We, as Christians, do not have to be defeated by the Satan imp. Does not the Word say, "... greater is he that is in you, than he that is in the world" (I John 4:4). The latter portion of the eighth chapter of Romans concludes with a mighty statement: "Nay, in all these things we are more than conquerors through him that loved us. For I am persuaded, that neither death, nor life, nor angels, nor principalities, nor powers, nor things present, nor things to come. Nor height, nor depth, nor any other creature, shall be able to separate us from the love of God, which is in Christ Jesus our Lord" (Romans 8:37-39). I John 5:4 says, "For whatsoever is born of God overcometh by the world..." Just like the incorruptible seed of the Word, by which we are born again, we live and abide forever (I Peter 1:23). In John, the 10th chapter, the writer records these words of Jesus: "And I give unto them eternal life; and they shall never perish, neither shall any man pluck them out of my hand. My father, which gave them me, is greater than all..." (John 10:28, 29).

3

Born to be King

The story is told of the Dauphin, an heir to the throne of France. The young man, at an early age, was torn from the company of those who loved and protected him, and was taken captive by a howling mob of ravaging, maniacal people. Someone in the crowd said, "Let's kill him!" Others nodded in agreement and that seemed to be the best idea until someone substituted another suggestion. "No," remonstrated this individual, "I have a better idea. Let's take this young man and turn him over to an old hag, a witch by the name of Meg. Let her blacken the heart and mind of this youngster." The crowd responded with enthusiastic agreement.

So the young Dauphin was placed in the hands of this diabolical, wretched woman. She taught him to steal and plunder, to rummage the garbage heaps of the city of Paris. But occasionally, when this vile woman would make wretched demands that were even more sordid than usual, something would rise up in the heart of this youngster. Having been taught by tutors at the court in earlier days, there was laying dormant in the subconscious of his soul those mighty ideals that would surface on occasion. On these occasions, the young Dauphin would defy the curses and commands of that vile, despicable character when she would force him to lie and curse and steal. Standing defiantly, he would lift his hands in protestation and cry, "I will not! I will not! I will not! I was born to be a king!"

This is what God intended for His creation. We were not created to walk in the earth embittered and overcome with the power of sin. We were created with a God-shaped blank in our souls that can never be filled with the misshapen application of worldly things. We were, rather, created to rise to the heights of eternal glory and fulfillment. God's promise through Isaiah still stands: "But they that wait upon the Lord shall renew their strength; they shall mount up with wings as eagles, they shall run, and not be weary; and they shall walk, and not faint" (Isaiah 40:31). Our original inheritance, our eternal destiny was meant to be kingship.

But what have we found in the beginning of the 3rd chapter of Genesis? Man is in a foul state. God had crowned His six days of re-creation with the creation of man. The brightest soul, the crown jewel of the planet earth was man. Man – crowned with the glory of the Almighty; walking in the splendor of heavenly light. But when Satan walked into the Garden of Eden and seduced man through the avenue of the serpent, a sad, black day entered into the universe. The sun of righteousness became blackened as though draped with a veil of mourning. The light of pristine holiness seemed to have been blown out. This hour was so black, that Paul wrote incisively in Romans 5:12 of this terrible hour: "Wherefore, as by one man sin entered into the world, and death by sin; and so death passed upon all men, for that all have sinned."

Think about it! Man had refused to bend his life to the God who made him. He refused to walk in the way of the truth and the light. He rejected the commandment of God – singular in this present instance. The sole commandment

that was given to man was rejected; the one provision
that God had given to man was spurned. The Bible gives a
number of strong hints as to what the future state of Adam
would have been had he proven himself. Surely he would
have been transformed from "glory to glory" (II Corinthians
3:18), that is, from the marvelous level he had been created
in to the level God's ultimate will intended for him to attain.

As we look at the creation story, and the subsequent
fall of man and woman, we ask, "Why, did not God kill the
devil? Then why did not God just annihilate man and begin
all over again?" The question has profound theological
overtones, and it probably is an unanswerable question,
since God has not chosen to reveal the answer. However,
certain facts cannot be overlooked. First, God created man
because the very nature of the Spirit Being, God, is "love."
And, although as St. Augustine tells us there was in the very
nature of the Trinity a lover, a beloved, and a spirit of love,
yet there seemed to be demand for an external creature who
could also respond with love.

Secondly, we might suggest that if God had created a
new system of spirit beings (angels), He would have been
confronted with the same risk He underwent when Lucifer
and the fallen host were originally created. And man, with
a free will, would have posed the same problems for God.
God thought the creation of angels and men worth the risk.
He, obviously, anticipated all the alternatives and proceeded
with His master plan for a heavenly kingdom on earth.

But we have been brought to the sorry state of
mankind. A once proud, beautiful pair of creatures are now
standing in the rubble of a once beautiful Garden of Eden.
Man, whose body could have existed eternally, has been
denied access to the tree of life. In my mind's eye I see

similar specimens of Adam and Eve on earth today. I see an Adam, a young man, who was once a robust specimen in the train of Charles Atlas; but I see him now, after sin has eaten with its cancerous venom into his body: but now he is but the brittle remains of a once strong, handsome young man. I see fallen Eve in a young lady who thought that sex and drugs was the fun way, the way to have kicks. But young people, illicit sex and debilitating drugs will give a "kick," but never forget that drinking at the fountain of the devil's pleasures will always have its "kickbacks." And what a heart-breaking picture: once rosy checks, and lustrous hair, and sparkling eyes, now turned into the sunken jaws, and bent body, that show the ravages of sin. That is where the devil has led men. Those whom Satan said would "become as gods," have become a godless, fallen, judgment bound race of unregenerate people.

What a sad picture that is! No home – driven from the Garden; no God – fellowship with the Almighty broken; no eternal life – death the only sure thing. What a sad, hopeless picture. And the philosophers of "no hope" (they call them existentialists and their doctrine "nihilism") are still painting this picture to mankind. I think the philosopher Goethe expressed it very well when he said, "If you have any certainties, let us have them. We have doubts enough of our own." We might paraphrase that to say, "If you have any hopes let us have them, we have enough despair of our own."

Thank God, we have that hope right here in the third chapter of Genesis. The heart of God comes through visibly and certainly. God did not destroy man, because He is a God of mercy, of kindness and of love. Those words of Simon Peter still stand: "The Lord is not slack concerning his promise, as some men count slackness; but is longsuffering to us-ward, not willing that any should perish, but that all should come to repentance" (II Peter 3:9). Up to the third chapter of Genesis, we have known God as the Creator, the Almighty. We picture Him as the "Logos," the Word, whose very speech brings untold universes into being. But now the nature of God that has been previously unrevealed strides forth: He is a God of love; a God of mercy; a God of loving-kindness.

Yes, neighbor, God is more that what the theologians like to call "the First Cause" or the "Unmoved Mover." A person could deal in theological speculations and abstractions about God that leave you cold, and spiritless, and lifeless. But you cannot excel I John 4:8: "God is love." That was **power** when God called forth the heavens and earth "from nothing" (ex nihilo), and by a mere spoken word this universe leaped into being. That was **ingenuity** when God fashioned man from the dust of the earth. That was **supreme intelligence** when God formed an orderly universe where heavenly orbs floated in absolute precision, and the universe obeyed the inexorable laws of God. That was **architectural splendor** and **beauty unparalleled** when God fashioned a garden where thorns and thistles did not grow and man and beast could dwell together in peace and harmony. That was **condescension** (to assume equality with an inferior) when God came down from the lofty heights of eternity and "walk in the garden in the cool of the day" and "called unto man. But, that was **love** that provided a "Lamb slain from the foundation of the world" (Revelation 13:8) who would save men from their sins (Matthew 1:21).

The Bible tells us: "For God so loved the world, that he gave his only begotten Son, that whosoever believeth in him should not perish, but have everlasting life. For God sent not his Son into the world to condemn the world; but that the world through him might be saved. He that believeth on him is not condemned: but he that believeth not is condemned already, because he hath not believed in the name of the only begotten Son of God" (John 3:16-18). And we read in Romans 5:19: "For as by one man's disobedience many were made sinners, so by the obedience of one shall many be made righteous."

Yes, my friend, right here in the early part of the blessed Book, God offers a provision for man's redemption from sin. Genesis 3:15 says, "And I will put enmity between thee and the woman, and between thy seed and her seed; it shall bruise thy head, and thou shalt bruise his heel." Here we find what is called the *"protevangelium,"* that is, "the first gospel." What does that mean? It means Calvary; it means the bloody sacrifice of a man on an old rugged cross. It meant the coming of a babe into the earth; a God-man – a Divine Spirit clothed in human flesh. It meant the awful ordeal of a man undergoing the cruel Roman-imposed torture of death on a cross. It meant the display of open shame of the Son of God on that hill called Golgotha. It meant that through the "deception of a woman" (Eve) a hideous, awful, terrible sin came into the world; but that also through the "conception of a woman" (Mary), the redemption of mankind from that sin also came into the world. Right here, embedded in what has been called by many Bible scholars the most important chapter of the whole of Scriptures (perhaps excluding John chapter 3), is the seed-plot of God's divine purpose for the redemption and restoration of mankind.

And there in the Garden of Eden, the Lord covered over the nakedness of man and woman. Then, He confronted that Serpent, the Devil, and spoke in this manner: "O serpent, the seed of the woman (the woman Eve – whom you deceived and through whom you have brought sin into the world) will crush your head – will bring mortal injury into your being." Encompassed in that verse is a declaration by God of the end of Satan, as well as a conflict which will rage between him and the righteous seed of the woman.

But there is something else in that verse. It is said that the old rabbis would pour over this verse seeking to understand what God meant when He spoke to Satan. What is this "seed of the woman?" Everyone knows that seed is masculine; seed belongs to a man, not a woman. Yes, that verse has long range reference to the Redeemer-Christ, who would suffer momentarily – a wound in the heel (the temporary defeat of Christ on Calvary) – but only to accomplish a permanent defeat for the devil: a wound to the head – speaking of mortal injury. It looks forward to that day when he and his impish hosts will be cast into Gehenna (the lake of fire) at the end-time. It is normal for the Scriptures to mention a progenitor as being in the masculine gender. Man, in this case, is nowhere mentioned, compelling the conclusion that Jehovah here had specific reference to the virgin mother of Christ in mind.

This same gospel of redemption is prefigured in verse 21 of this third chapter. We read, "Unto Adam and to his wife did the Lord God make coats of skins, and clothed them." Here is a picture of unregenerate man. What did he do when he found himself naked? (Raw nakedness, exposure in a public sense, is a picture of the unregenerate man; even Adam had not deteriorated so completely that his sensibilities and social amenities were totally blighted. He, at least, wanted to clothe himself. Did not the demoniac, when healed of his mental stupor, became restored to his right mind and clothe himself.) But man gathered fig leaves and sewed them together. And ever since, man apart from God has been attempting to clothe himself spiritually with the fragile, decaying, manmade frocks of self-reform and self-righteousness.

Fig leaves, man's self-made escape mechanism from a guilty conscience, will not hide nor cover up a heart that is desperately wicked and far gone from righteousness. A man can pile up his charitable and philanthropic endeavors; he can boast of his religiosity – but from the 3rd chapter of Genesis, to the concluding book of Revelation, it is still "Worthy is the Lamb that was slain" (Revelation 5:12). All our worthiness is unworthiness before the worthy Lamb.

Yes, somewhere in the Garden of Eden God slew the first sacrificial victim, an innocent animal that prefigured the greater sacrifice of Jesus Christ on Calvary. Somewhere in the inner recesses of that beautiful garden, the ground drank the blood of an innocent creature. And what a beautiful, significant picture as God makes a coat to cover the shame and nakedness of Adam and Eve. And, doctrinally, what a delightful picture: a foretaste of the atonement (the covering of our sins), and the washing away of our sins by shed blood. I never tire of singing that great song that says:

> *"What can wash away my sins?*
> *Nothing but the blood of Jesus;*
> *What can make me whole again?*
> *Nothing but the blood of Jesus.*
> *Chorus: Oh! Precious is the flow,*

That makes me white as snow;
No other fount I know,
Nothing but the blood of Jesus."

Man was then driven from the garden with these words: "And the Lord God said, Behold, the man is become as one of us, to know good and evil: and now, lest he put forth his hand, and take also of the tree of life, and eat, and live forever: therefore the Lord God sent him forth from the Garden of Eden, to till the ground from whence he was taken. So he drove out the man; and he placed at the east of the Garden of Eden Cherubims, and a flaming sword which turned every way, to keep the way of the tree of life" (Genesis 3:22-24). The tree of life is taken away lest man should eat and live forever: meaning that man would have lived forever in his fallen, degenerate, sinful, decaying, perishing body for all eternity. He would have retained a body subject to hurt and sickness and ills; all that sinful flesh is heir to. But God mercifully spared man this eternal ruin.

We do not care to talk about death; but death is often a release. One who has suffered so long is often released from the pangs of suffering by death. The Book of revelation speaks of those who sought death and could not find it. How many saints have become resigned to the will of God and have come to believe that perhaps death would be a better solution for a suffering loved one (natural death, not euthanasia). Perhaps death would be a release from the toil and strife of this world, should God choose not to heal a loved one.

At the east of the Garden God placed Cherubims. Now these Cherubims stand as a monument telling man that there is a way to return to Paradise. Cherubims in the Bible

are always symbols of divine mercy and grace. In the holy
of holies they were atop the ark of the covenant, standing
on either side of the mercy seat, their eyes full upon it and
their wings covering it. Between them flamed the Shekinah,
the fire of the glory of God. To this place came the High
Priest with the blood of the atonement, and there the mercy
and forgiveness of God met the repentance and confession
of man. And reconciliation between man and God was
effected.

Friend, here in the "first Gospel," God is offering a way
of return. Those Cherubims still stand with outstretched
arms, symbolizing a way of return. God's grace still abounds
to a heart that is awakened from its condition of despair.
We were born to be "kings" and citizens of God's eternal
kingdom.

4

Kill the Spider

An old deacon who was always called upon to pray at the Wednesday night prayer service would customarily conclude his prayer with these words: "And, Lord, clean all the cobwebs out of my life." The cobwebs were those things that had gathered during the week, but which should not have been there. One fellow, who also attended midweek service regularly, got irritated at this fellow for his repetitive statement about the cobweb. On the particular Wednesday night in question, the deacon concluded with his customary benediction. Whereupon, the fellow jumped to his feet and shouted: "Lord, don't do it! Kill the spider!"

Too often Christians are engaged in a fruitless, but never ending, cleaning of the cobwebs out of their lives. But total, complete victory will never come until we deal with the true source of our problems. We are approached from three directions; spiders attempt to spin their webs in three different ways. Therefore, we must be wary of the wiles of the devil, and we must be observant of his schemes.

As we pointed out earlier, man is a tripartite (three-part) creature. One has to go no farther than the second chapter of Genesis to arrive at this conclusion. Genesis 2:7 says, "And the Lord God formed man of the dust of the ground, and breathed into his nostrils the breath of life; and man became a living soul." This verse tells us that man's body was made from the dust of the ground. Then the spirit was given to man as the breath of God. And the combining of these two, body and spirit, produced the soul. Thus I might say that, "I am soul and spirit; I have a body. No matter what distinctions may be made between soul and spirit, man has, clearly, a physical and a spiritual nature; a corporeal and an incorporeal nature.

The soul becomes that part of man which gives him self-consciousness. Many people are not aware of this but animals, other than man, have a soul. Over twenty times the word is used for the lower animals, thus showing that they have a soul, although they do not have spirits. Man is a soul and as such he has his own identity; he is constituted an individual thereby. And since animals have souls, each one of those creatures has his own identity as well. Thus the Lord pointed out that "The foxes have holes, and the birds of the air have nests" (Matthew 8:20). And, not surprisingly, each animal goes to his own lair or nest or home at the appointed time of rest.

But the soul, which is the self, the ego, (the "I" of psychology), has a "spirit." The original state of the spirit consisted of the breath ("pneuma") being blown into man. This spirit was breathed into him when he was created, and this spirit distinguishes man from the animals of the forest. Hardly any man would deny that man is essentially a religious creature. The great St. Augustine said that man was created for fellowship with God and he is never at rest until he finds rest in Him.

Now some theologians fail to distinguish between soul and spirit (trichotomy and dichotomy). But we must do so in order to understand what happened to man. The old holiness writers said that man was created body, soul, and a spirit. And when Adam sinned, God withdrew His Holy Spirit from man, and the spirit of man crumbled and became darkened by sin. Consequently, man is "dead in trespasses and sins" (Ephesians 2:11). Paul wrote that the natural man "receiveth not the times of the spirit of God" (I Corinthians 2:14).

Oh, but what happens when I get saved, when I am born again? When the image of God is renewed at a crisis point in man's life, he becomes a new creature. God, through His Holy Spirit, plants a new spirit within man and he can cry, "old things are passed away; all things are become new" (II Corinthians 5:17). The spirit gives me God-consciousness.

Thirdly, man has a body. When death comes, the body falls, but the soul and spirit return to their maker. The body returns to the dust from whence the first body had been created. But while man lives in the body, the body gives him a world consciousness. It makes him a sentient, feeling being. It makes him responsive to the things that are about him. With eyes he sees; with ears he hears; with the mouth he speaks; with legs he walks; with hands he feels; and with the tongue he tastes, and so on.

This discussion brings us to a salient point: Man has three basic areas that are vulnerable to attack from Satan. Against the body he brings the temptations of the flesh. Against the soul he brings the temptations of the world. And against the spirit, Satan himself, or through one of his lesser agents, seek to win over the worship of man, and turn man against God. A renowned evangelist often says, "Locate your enemy!"

"Locate your enemy!" "Why locate your enemy?"
Because we must know from which direction he is coming.
The place and method of attack will determine the weapons
we must use against our enemy. Hence, the success of our
spiritual warfare will depend greatly upon our understanding
of the three areas of attack, and our determination of the
kind of spiritually appointed warfare we are going to use to
defend ourselves.

Let us look at our defense by considering the area of
the "flesh." The term "flesh" ('sarx' in the original Greek)
is used in many ways in the New Testament. Sometimes it
simply means that material which covers our bones. Jesus
used the term "flesh" in this manner when He spoke in Luke
24:39: "Behold my hands and my feet, that it is I myself:
handle me, and see; for a spirit hath not flesh and bones,
as ye see me have." And then, flesh is used to represent
the whole body (Acts 2:26), and again, in the sense of our
physical, earthly limitations (II Corinthians 10:3, 4).

But flesh is sometimes used in a sense other than the
soft fleshly substance that covers the bones. This flesh
we have been discussing is not sinful – not the body itself.
But the word "flesh" used in a symbolic sense denotes the
earthly part of man apart from God, and devoted in its uses
to sinful pursuits. And that flesh, dominated by the power of
sin, can sprout a multitude of sinful qualities. This is what
the apostle Paul talked about when he wrote in Galatians:
"The acts of the sinful nature are obvious: sexual immorality,
impurity and debauchery; idolatry and witchcraft; hatred,
discord, jealousy, fits of rage, selfish ambition, dissensions,
factions and envy; drunkenness, orgies, and the like. I
warn you, as I did before, that those who live like this will

not inherit the kingdom of God." (Galatians 5:19-21, New International Version).

Jesus told us a lot about this flesh in Mark the 7th chapter. The Pharisees were castigating the disciples for their ceremonial uncleanness. Pharisees were scrupulous in their ritualistic observances. They meticulously washed their hands and their vessels, thinking that making the outside of the platter clean took care of the filthiness on the inside of the platter. Or they believed that the washing of the hands sufficed for purification of the heart. What did Jesus do? He reprimanded them severely when He said, "There is nothing from without a man, that entering into him can defile him: but the things which come out of him, those are they that defile the man!" (Mark 7:15). Also, "For from within, out of the heart of men, proceed evil thoughts, adulteries, fornications, murders, thefts, covetousness, wickedness, deceit, lasciviousness, an evil eye, blasphemy, pride, foolishness. All these evil things come from within, and defile the man" (Mark 7:21-23).

Now, as a Christian what am I going to do in order to beat the flesh? In order to overcome the flesh? Paul met the problem head-on in Romans. He told those people that "... where sin abounded, grace did much more abound" (Romans 5:20). Some inquirers must have interpreted that to mean: the more I sin the more grace I have. So Paul refuted such thinking when he said, "What shall we say then? Shall we continue in sin, that grace may abound? God forbid. How shall we that are dead to sin, live any longer therein? Know ye not, that so many of us as were baptized into Jesus Christ were baptized into his death? Therefore we are buried with him by baptism into death: that like as Christ was raised up from the dead by the glory of the Father, even so we also should walk in newness of life. For if we have been planted together in the likeness of his resurrection: Knowing this, that our old man is crucified with him, that the body of sin might be destroyed, that henceforth we should not serve sin. For he that is dead is freed from sin" (Romans 6:1-7).

The Word for destroyed in verse 6 is from the Greek word *"kartegeo"* meaning to "make void, or to make none effect." The power that caused the flesh to pour out sinful expressions is devitalized. Reformation will not do it: turning over a new leaf will not do it – because the next little wind of adversity that comes along will turn it back over. It takes a godly inclination wherein one can say, "It is 'not I, but Christ liveth in me'" (Galatians 2:20).

Now we must understand a second point which many Christians fail to grasp. It is true that the "flesh" used symbolically as the body under the dominion of sin, may be broken in its power to serve man to commit the sins of the flesh. That is, it is crucified, it is dead. But the "flesh," the body through which temptations knock upon our door, is just alive as it ever was. I do gain a great victory when the flesh, the body under the dominion of sinful motivations, is crucified, but the body of material flesh still remains; and just as surely as I exist, this body can be tempted and tried. And the man that thinks that he has gained eternal victory over the flesh should take heed to the Scripture that says, "So, if you think you are standing firm, be careful that you don't fall" (I Corinthians 10:12, New International Version). Self-righteous assurance will get one into trouble.

When the Bible speaks of the temptations of the flesh, it is always in terms of a continued need to overcome them. We never achieve a total victory of freedom "from" temptation; but by the power of the Holy Spirit we achieve a victory of freedom "over" temptations that continually beset us. Galatians 5:16 says, "This I say then, Walk in the Spirit, and ye shall not fulfill the lust of the flesh." Note: It does not say that you will not "have" temptations if you walk in the Spirit; but, rather, that if you walk in the Spirit you will not fulfill those temptations.

Temptations will still come when you get sanctified (even according to the old-time holiness advocates). Temptation and sin are not the same thing. The old cliché says, "You cannot stop a bird from landing on your head, but you can stop it from building a nest in your hair." You cannot stop the devil from knocking on your door, but you do not have to invite him in.

Here is the key word for the Christian: Flight. Even after crucifixion of the flesh, young man and young lady, the Bible gives us a further admonition: "Flee also youthful lust" (II Timothy 2:22). And the same Bible says, "Flee fornication" (I Corinthians 6:18). And the same Word says, "abstain from fleshly lusts, which war against the soul" (I Peter 2:11).

A young man was entrenched in one of the foxholes in France during World War I. The order was given to attack, but as the bombs began to explode and the bullets whizzed around his head, the boy became nervous and frightened. Throwing down his rifle, he began running toward the rear. The captain yelled, "Hey, John, where are you retreating to?" Hardly slackening his pace, the young fellow yelled over his shoulder, "Sir, I am not retreating: I am just 'advancing' to the rear." This is really what God wants you to do. By retreating and avoiding these sins you will, in reality, be advancing your Christian experience.

The second aspect of our great battle is the "world." Just what is the world? The Bible explanation may step on some of our cherished concepts about the definition of the word world. But we are, admittedly, concerned with the Scriptural definition and understanding in this matter. Unfortunately, too many Christians develop peevishness about their doctrines of the world. We must recognize that we can gain personal convictions on the subject of worldliness that do not necessarily appertain to other Christians (Romans 14:14; Titus 1:15).

Now, we do recognize that in many cases the world is becoming churchy, and the church is becoming worldly. We further agree that in some cases the early church was in the world, and the world is now too often in the church. We must also decry the assertion of those who contend that the church needs to catch the spirit of the age; rather, she needs to change the spirit of the age. The church will, in fact, only succeed as she corrects the worldliness that has infiltrated her pews and pulpits.

I know a fellow minister who was castigated by a parishioner in one of his pastorates. The well-meaning person complimented him on his preaching, however, he continued his exhortation by insisting that the preacher did not preach about sin in the manner that he should. The minister replied by saying, "Brother, I do not believe that I understand what you are talking about. I do believe in the awfulness of sin, and I believe I preach against sin." To his remonstrance the good man replied, "Oh, what I mean is **you don't name it!**" Unfortunately, we may get so caught up in our legalistic pursuits that we begin to catalogue "worldliness" to such an extent that we miss the meat of the definition of worldliness. Some Christian's catalogue of definitions of worldliness would put the Jewish Mishna to shame.

Now the term "world" (much like the term "flesh"), is used in the Bible in more than one way. First, the word "world" comes from the Greek "cosmos" which admits of several definitions: to order, arrangement and ornament or adornment. In the latter usage of the word we get our word "cosmetics," which is the concept of adorning the outer appearance.

Thus in the Bible the "world" is used in the sense of the planet earth, the material planet. In Acts 17:24 and John 1:10 we find this definition. Secondly, "world" is used to mean the inhabitants of the earth. No more blessed and comforting Scripture can be found in the Word than John 3:16, "For God so loved the world. ..." The world of mankind – God said He even loved them. The world that God loved was composed of believers and non-believers, good men and bad men. It was composed of those who were sons and daughters of Abraham, as well as those who were aliens from the commonwealth of God (John 14:17; 15:18).

But there is another usage of this word which is symbolic in nature. This is the usage that primarily concerns us. The word "world" is used to describe the "world system" that is so beautifully arranged and organized. But it is a system so arranged and functioning in such a manner, without God, that it has become opposed to everything that is good, godly, holy, pure and righteous.

As we pointed out earlier, that "world system" began in the Garden of Eden when Adam handed over his dominion of the earth to the Devil, and the Devil became the "god of this world." At that time there was injected into this universe a will and way contrary to God's will and way. And, significantly, it remains on this planet today.

That early world system under the direction of Satan developed so rapidly in its unrighteousness and evil that man became incorrigibly degenerate: "And God saw that the wickedness of man was great in the earth and that every imagination of the thoughts of his heart was only evil continually" (Genesis 6:5). Mister, that is what the Devil can do through the world system of evil. One of the saddest pictures in all of the Holy Writ is revealed by Paul, while in prison and with but a few friends, when he wrote to his son in the ministry Timothy: "For Demas hath forsaken me, having loved this present world ..." (II Timothy 4:10). A promising young minister hit the rocks when he allowed the world's siren call to beckon him.

An old Oxford English Dictionary describes the "world" as: "worldly affairs; the aggregate of things earthly; the whole circle of earthly goods, endowments, riches, advantages, pleasures, etc., which, although hollow and frail and fleeting, stir desire, seduce from God, and are obstacles to the cause of Christ." Over all this, Satan is the prince.

What is your "world?" I could not possibly know the answer to that question. The nature of your world may differ from the person nearest to you. It is true that it may not be the same. "Worldliness" is anything that keeps you from God. It is those things that become evil and idolatrous because you have adopted the attitudes and vices of the world system rather than the motives of the spiritual kingdom. When the devil cannot reach us through the temptations of the flesh, he will switch to the world system of seemingly innocent pursuits and things.

It is so easy to pull the affections of the world-system into our hearts. And in so doing, we push Christ and the Spirit out; they are so displaced as Lord and Master of our living. I see a father so caught up with the world-system of moneymaking, that he no longer works just to make a living. No, he lives to accumulate stocks and bonds and conveniences, and these become so important that he does not have time to attend church and give attention to Godly things. I see a wife so caught up with the world system of social activities, hobnobbing with the sophisticates of society, so that God has no place in her time. I see a young man so caught up with the whirl of social activities, and pleasure seeking that spiritual things have no place in his heart. I see a young lady so caught up in the world-system by the desire for marriage that God's plan for her life is rejected for her own self-willed desires.

What is worldliness? I will tell you what it is: it is entering into seemingly innocent things such as getting an education, making money, pursuing a career, obtaining fame, following the social circle, dating a girl or boy, seeking pleasure, or any of a multitude of other things – it is shifting these things from the world system into first place in your heart. It is letting these or any other things take priority and precedence over Christ and God and the Holy Spirit. Mister, it is prostituting the good on the altar of Satan, rather than climbing upon the altar of God and consecrating and sanctifying your time and your talents and your entire being to God. "Unto the pure all things are pure" (Titus 1:15), but "all things are not expedient" (profitable) (I Corinthians 10:23). We must not allow the seemingly innocent things of this world-system to dominate our hearts to such an extent that we allow them to push Christ into the background. Christ will either "be all" or we shall not have Christ "at all."

Hear the Word of God: Romans 12:1, 2 (The New English Bible): "Therefore, My Brothers, I implore you by God's mercy to offer your very selves to him: a living sacrifice, dedicated and fit for his acceptance, the worship offered by mind and heart. Adapt yourselves no longer to the pattern of this present world, but let your minds be remade and your whole nature thus transformed. Then you will be able to discern the will of God, and to know what is good, acceptable, and perfect." And the apostle John said, "Love not the world (system), neither the things that are in the world (system). If any man love the world (system), the love of the Father is not in him. For all that is in the world (system), the lust of the flesh, and the lust of the eyes, and the pride of life, is not of the Father, but is of the world (system). And the world (system) passeth away, and the lust thereof, but he that doeth the will of God abideth forever" (I John 2:15-17).

The world system of sensuality, good times, and pleasure will pass away, but the man that does the will of God will abide forever. A man asked Dwight L. Moody on one occasion, "How shall I give up the world?" Moody replied, "Brother, give a ringing testimony for God, and the world will give you up." We do not have to worry about the world capturing us if we are Spirit-filled and Christ-centered in our lives and testimonies. Jesus said, "If ye were of the world, the world would love his own: but because ye are not of the world, but I have chosen you out of the world, therefore the world hateth you" (John 15:19). Again, in John 17:14: "I have given them thy word; and the world hath hated them, because they are not of the world, even as I am not of the world." As long as we live, we cannot get out of the world, but neither should we be a part of it: "I pray thee, not to take them out of the world, but to keep them from the evil one. They are strangers in the world, as I am. Consecrate them by the truth; thy word is truth. As thou hast sent me into the world, I have sent them into the world, and for their sake I now consecrate myself, that they too may be consecrated by the truth" (John 17:15-19), The New English Bible).

You can be in the world, yet not of the world. The boat can be in the sea, and yet not have the sea in the boat. The fish can be in the water, and yet not have the water in the fish. When the water gets in the fish or the boat, watch out! We must live in the world, but when the world's values become a part of us, we get into trouble.

What is the key word in our defense against the world? **Faith!** "This is the victory that overcometh the world, even our faith!" (I John 5:4). Jesus said in John 18:36, "My kingdom is not of this world: if my kingdom were of this world, then would my servants fight, that I should not be delivered to the Jews: but now is my kingdom not from hence." Paul said, "For though we walk in the flesh, we do not war after the flesh: (For the weapons of our warfare are not carnal, but mighty through God to the pulling down of strongholds;) Casting down imaginations, and every high thing that exalteth itself against the knowledge of God, and bringing into captivity every thought to the obedience of Christ" (II Corinthians 10:3-5). James, also, warns against friendship with the world (James 4:4).

The third area of devious intrigue is under the direction of the Devil himself. We shall deal with this perpetrator of evil in more detail later on. But he and his demonic hordes seek to penetrate into the spirit-realm of man. Therefore, we are cautioned: "For we wrestle not against flesh and block, but against principalities, against powers against the rulers of the darkness of this world, against spiritual wickedness in high places. Wherefore take unto you the whole armor of God, that ye may be able to withstand in the evil day, and having done all, to stand. Stand therefore, having your loins girt about with truth, and having on the breastplate of righteousness; And your feet shod with the preparation of the gospel of peace; Above all, taking the shield of faith where with ye shall be able to quench all the fiery darts of the wicked. And take the helmet of salvation, and the sword of the Spirit, which is the word of God" (Ephesians 6:12-17).

The Devil wants to intrude into the spirit and take over; he wants to build up spiritual pride. The Devil seeks the blind to lead the blind; unbelieving churches to lead others astray with their "doctrines of devils" (I Timothy 4:1). The key word in our defense against the devil is **fight!** Put on the whole armor of God; gird up for a fight. I Timothy 6:12 says, "Fight the good fight of faith." And James 4:7 exhorts us to, "Resist the devil, and he will flee from you." God has given us an adequate defense against the wiles (cunning devices) of Satan.

5

The Beginning of the End

When we think about the great conflict between the Devil and God, the outcome is a foregone conclusion. On one hand, God in heaven has all wisdom, all knowledge, and all power; therefore, the inevitability of victory in the conflict is certain. The war which we have been mentioning in our lessons is certain as to its conclusion. God knows an event even before it happens; and He knows the conclusion of it before it is begun.

The death of Jesus on the cross was the death knell to the kingdom of Satan, and all its philosophies and principles of operation. During World War II some of us remember hearing the commentators describe certain battle victories, such as the landing on the Normandy Coast in France, as "the beginning of the end." These battles, in other words, were so decisive, that the end was only a matter of time away. Thus the battle of the cross, the victory that Jesus won on Calvary, was the beginning of the end – it was so decisive that Satan's final demise would come in only a matter of time. It seems as though an angel stands on the edge of eternity and cries: "Forasmuch then as the children are partakers of flesh and blood, he also himself likewise took part of the same; that through death he might destroy him that had the power of death, that is, the devil" (Hebrews 2:14).

However, it is true that our fight as believers has not yet come to an end. It is true that the Sovereign God has predestined certain things to take place, and has made provision for the fulfillment of others. But have you not prayed many times the Lord's Prayer, particularly that verse which says, "Thy kingdom come. Thy will be done in earth as it is in heaven" (Matthew 6:10). God is yet working out on earth those great principles which the Trinitarian council has decreed in heaven. God has foreordained certain events in the Bible just as though they had taken place. After all, He sees the beginning from the end. He knows the conclusion of every matter which has ever been begun. His prophet has said, "For my thoughts are not your thoughts, neither are your ways my ways" (Isaiah 55:8). But God has said it, and we must believe it.

So it is that the world stands in dismay at the cross. Paul said, "For the preaching of the cross is to them that perish foolishness, but unto us which are saved it is the power of God" (I Corinthians 1:18). The world simply cannot understand the power of the cross; man in his carnal state is simply overwhelmed by its purpose and truths. To the man who has no faith, the cross is the most absurd, monumental disaster known to mankind. And for Christians to rejoice in that emblem of shame seems rather foolish. But Christians recognize the condition of the worldly man: "Having eyes, see ye not, and having ears, hear ye not?" (Mark 8:18). But the child of God, through the power of the Holy Spirit, has had them "revealed... unto us" (I Corinthians 2:10). Yes, the cross of Christ stands supreme, first of all, because it took away the curse of the law. Now the law was not a bad thing. Sometimes we look upon the law as something awful and sinful. Not so! The law was neither unholy nor sinful. Paul said in Romans 7:12. "Wherefore the law is holy..." and in verse 14, "For we know that the law is spiritual: but I am carnal, sold under sin." The law was the most perfect commandment ever given to mankind. The thunders and lightning of Sinai bespeak of the righteous judgment that falls on the violators of that holy law. Sinful flesh and dishonorable hearts must tremble before the righteous demands of the law.

But what was the "curse" of the law? We can, perhaps, sum it up by the following statement. The law was not given to be kept, it was given to be broken. And when we break the law, the law, in turn, breaks us. The law could be likened to a schoolmaster who lashes, and drives, and teaches. The law was a mirror that reflects the imperfections of our lives. The law was perfect and, of necessity, must reflect the imperfectness of every son of Adam who ever stood before it. Summarily, the law was not given to redeem or save us, it was given to break and reveal us. "Wherefore the law was our schoolmaster to bring us unto Christ, that we might be justified by faith" (Galatians 3:24).

Here we stand today: the love of God in Christ took my Saviour to the cross, where He paid the penalty to satisfy the claims of a holy God. There a full, vicarious, substitutionary atonement was made for my sins and He gave full satisfaction for the law's claims upon my life by becoming my Saviour. What I could not do, Jesus did on Calvary. The debt I could not pay, Jesus "paid it all." The claims of the law I could not satisfy, Jesus satisfied them all. The law I could not disannul, Jesus disannulled on Calvary.

Therefore, I can proclaim, "There is therefore no condemnation to them which are in Christ Jesus, who walk not after the flesh, but after the Spirit" (Romans 8:1). My judgment (condemnation) as a child of God is past history. I can proclaim with Christ "It is finished" (John 19:30). The purpose of God is complete, the plan of redemption has been completed, and everything that it took to satisfy a holy and just God has been completed. The curse of the law has been done away with and now I can sing: "Near the Cross, O Lamb of God, Bring its scenes before me; Help me walk from day to day, With its shadows o'er me! Near the Cross, a trembling soul, Love and mercy found me: There the Bright and Morning Star, Shed its beams around me! Near the Cross I'll watch and wait, Hoping, trusting ever, Till I reach the golden strand, Just beyond the river!" Hear me! The judgment by the law of the believer is past; the question of the law's ability to crush and curse is gone. The believer looks forward to nothing but eternal bliss and eternal salvation with His God. The only judgment a believer will face is a judgment of rewards, in which he will be abundantly rewarded for his faithfulness and service to God.

Who was it that put Jesus Christ on the cross to bear the curse of the law? It was not the power of the Sanhedrin court; neither was it the political might of the Roman Empire. It was not the Gentiles, nor the populace, nor the rabble – neither was it the executioners who drove those spikes into his flesh and raised that crude cross to a standing position on the top of Golgotha. No! But it was by the foreknowledge and permissive will of my God that He was brought to the palace. Peter said in the Pentecost sermon, "Him, being delivered by the determinate counsel and foreknowledge of God..." (Acts 2:23). Isaiah has said it a long time ago, "Yet it pleased the lord to bruise him..." (Isaiah 53:10). God, in fact, "sent" His Son. The song says, "He could have called ten-thousand angels. ..." And he could have. He could have mustered myriads of the heavenly hosts; or he could have spoken a word as He did when He called the cosmos into existence, and that spoken word could have banished the world and all its iniquitous inhabitants to oblivion.

But not so. He chose another way; He chose the will of the Father when he prayed, "... not my will, but thine, be done" (Luke 22:42). And, "Christ hath redeemed us from the curse of the law, being made a curse for us: for it is written, Cursed is every one that hangeth on a tree" (Galatians 3:13). And that marvelous passage in II Corinthians 5:21, "For he hath made him to be sin for us, who knew no sin" that we might be made the righteousness of God in him." He became our "sacrifice for sin" when He died on the cross, and removed the curse and judgment of the law from the believer. No friend, the cross was not, as some men believe, an erasure, and eradication, a subtraction of a just and righteous man – rather, it stands as heaven's + sign in an otherwise less than desirable world. It is the ultimate, the zenith, the apex, the epitome of divine mercy and condescension to man.

The cross of Jesus Christ was, in fact, a revelation of God's way in contrast to the ways of the devil. Men try to follow the secular, sinful, Satanic inspired system of this world. We can sum it up in "selfishness" – God's ways are not man's ways. This is a truth that is not proclaimed often enough. "There is a way which right unto a man, but the end thereof are the ways of death" (Proverbs 14:12). The foolishness of the cross, and the humility of Christ by dying on that cross, has forever shown the selfish, fallen philosophy of Satan to be corrupt and degenerate. It was, and is, the great expose of the pattern of earthliness and sinfulness as an incorrect method of attaining heaven.

That ignominious death of Christ on Calvary has been an example that has tarnished the good words of every self-righteous, self-aspiring man of every century since then. The cross may be compared to a big mirror; every time sinful man looks into it, his prideful, sinful ways are shown to be what they really are: devices of Satan. The old cliché says, "You ought to be ashamed of yourself." There it is – every sinner ought to be ashamed of himself or herself. "When I survey the wondrous cross, on which the Prince of glory died, My richest gain I count but loss, And pour contempt on all my pride."

The hollow, frail ways of this world will not hold up before the unpretentious humility of the lowly man of Galilee. Jesus had stung the Pharisees when He said, "But all their works they do for to be seen of men: they make broad their phylacteries, and enlarge the borders of their garments" (Matthew 23:5). Thus Jesus has exposed the world, and the world system. Now He was using the cross to incapacitate the deceiver's power to use the law, and now He was also going to use the cross to disarm him altogether.

Listen to Colossians 2:15: "On that cross he discarded the cosmic powers and authorities like a garment; he made a public spectacle of them and led them as captives in his triumphal procession" (New English Translation). The King James Version says that He "spoiled principalities and powers." Satan has misused the office that was granted Him by God before the creation of this earth. He had usurped the prerogative and rights from Adam and Eve. And God, even though still Sovereign in this universe, had recognized

Satan's right to exercise a certain amount of freedom in this direction. But now, at the cross, Jesus was wresting from Satan all these things, and was initiating the "beginning of the end." John saw the conclusion to the matter and reported it in Revelation 11:15: "And the seventh angel sounded; and there were great voices in heaven, saying, the kingdoms of this world are becoming the kingdoms of our Lord, and of his Christ; and he shall reign forever and ever."

It was true that Satan gained such an opportunity to enter the world's affairs that after the fall of Adam the Scriptures referred to him with terminology that recognized his authority. He was called "the god of this age" (II Corinthians 4:4); the "prince of this world" (John 12:31); the "prince of the power of the air" (Ephesians 2:2); the head of "the rulers of the darkness of this world" (Ephesians 6:12). But God, as we mentioned earlier, was making a provision to wrest this power from this pretender and evil fomenter. The cross, in the mind of God, was to be not only the great equalizer, but the superior weapon, as it were, to bring a conclusion to the whole enterprise. Oh, those centuries of delay; those periods of drought when it seemed that neither the voice of God nor of His prophets was to be heard anywhere in the land. It is true that "the mills of God grind slowly, but they grind sure." Time was moving towards a certain conclusion just as God has willed for it to.

The first stage in that inevitable conclusion toward which that world was moving was an immediate release of the captive spirits in Paradise. When Jesus hung suspended on that cross beneath those Syrians skies, He had assured one of the two thieves that, "Today shalt thou be with me in paradise" (Luke 23:43). When the body of my Saviour hung limp and lifeless on the cross, the Spirit of Christ departed that tabernacle of clay and He descended (Ephesians 4:9) into hell (Hades: the realm of the departed spirits of both good and bad people.) This place was divided by a great gulf fixed; one side contained righteous men, and was called "Abraham's bosom" (Luke 16:22) or "Paradise" (Luke 23:43). It was here that Jesus invaded a territory that Satan had claimed for his own, and took from him a power that, up to this time, was both awesome and fearsome.

It is here that we find one of the most tremendous truths in all of time and eternity: "Forasmuch then as the children are partakers of flesh and blood, he also himself likewise took part of the same: that through death he might destroy him that had the power of death, that is, the devil" (Hebrews 2:14). Jesus destroyed, rendered useless, worthless, this power that Satan was even permitted to use on occasion to bring about the physical death of a believer (I Corinthians 5:5). But now Jesus walked into that place that Satan claimed, and when he had "descended first into the lower parts of the earth" (Ephesians 4:9), then he stood as the victor over death. John the Revelator later saw Him in heaven as He proclaimed: "I am he that liveth, and was dead; and, behold, I am alive for evermore, Amen; and have the keys of hell and of death" (Revelation 1:18).

My Lord marched down the corridors of Paradise and proclaimed liberty to a vast host of Old Testaments Saints who had looked toward the coming of Messiah by faith (Hebrews 13). When Jesus strolled forth from Paradise with the keys of death attached to His girdle, he had an entourage of followers who vacated that place. So complete was that victory that God allowed a select company of those believers to acquire resurrection bodies. Matthew 27:52, 53, says "And the graves were opened; and many bodies of the saints which slept arose. And came out of the graves after his resurrection, and went into the holy city, and appeared unto many." We often sing an old gospel song that says:

> *"When the redeemed, are gathering in,*
> *Washed like snow, and free from all sin,*
> *How we will shout, and how we will sing,*
> *When the redeemed are gathering in."*

This little group of people were the first fruits, a foretaste of an innumerable host of God's sons and daughters who shall ascend with Him in the last day. Hebrew 2:10 says, "For it became him, for whom are all things, and by whom are all things, in bringing many sons unto glory, to make the captain of their salvation perfect through sufferings." The cross, then, was not the eradication of the Son of God; it was the eradication of the Devil. It brought to fruition the plan of God, superseded the power of the enemy, and offered to all men of faith a great hope. Those who believe in His wonderful name shall one day judge the world (I Corinthians 6:2), judge the angels (I Corinthians 6:3), and shall sit upon the throne of our Saviour (Revelation 3:21).

*One of the most irritating things that can happen to a
person is to go up to a fountain when he is really thirsty,
turn the knob, and find no water issues forth. But this is
not so with God. Jesus promised His people a well of living
water that would never run dry. From where do we get our
strength? From the well, the living water, the power of His
Presence that strengthens, energizes, and sustains us in
those moments of need.*

6

What Meaneth This?

*A*nd they were all amazed... saying... Behold, are not all these which speak Galileans? And how hear we every man in our own tongue...? What meaneth this? (Acts 2:7, 8, 12).

Curiosity and vigorous debate have surrounded one of the most notable and important doctrines of the entire Word of God. It is to those who are not acquainted with the meaning of this blessed experience, that I wish to address myself. Surely every sincere, Bible believing Christian has an obligation to search the Scriptures and to come to an understanding of the meaning of Pentecost and the Holy Spirit blessing that is promised in these days to God's people.

The hue and cry of many when they first become acquainted with, or hear about, those who emphasize the Pentecostal blessing is: "What meaneth this?" or, "What is this all about?" I met a man not many months ago who had just received the fullness of the Spirit. His eyes glistened as he talked about this newfound joy; his face radiated a spiritual glow as he spoke of this new spiritual experience. But it was with a degree of amazement that I heard him tell of twenty or so years spent in a Christian church, with periodic readings of the great passages from the Acts of the Apostles, and yet, until recently, he had never really understood or experienced the real meaning of Pentecostal power.

I would never cast stones at my Christian brethren. We are all subject to the realm of which Paul spoke, when he said, "Now we see through a glass darkly, but then face to face." In a sense we are all seeking for deeper depths and striving to reach higher heights of spiritual attainment. But perhaps we shall, this morning, be able to lead you a little further into a biblical understanding of this vital subject as we attempt to answer the question, "What meaneth this?"

Men are always amazed at the acts of God. Nearly 2,000 years ago 120 men and women were gathered in an upper room. These followers of the late Galilean, Jesus, were, by and large, people without any great advantage in life. They were not wealthy, or well educated, or endowed with social prestige. Yet, as we look into that room through the second widow of Acts, we see this unlettered, unlearned group of men and women speaking in languages from many countries the world over. Manifestations of divine power were all about them. Lambent, forked tongues of fire were seen to fall upon them. The uninitiated and uninformed must have wondered at the apparent confusion and bedlam in that upper room.

Unfortunately, people judge the modern Pentecostal movement in the same light. First Cor. 3:19 says, "For the wisdom of this world is foolishness with God." We might add that God's wisdom and works are often foolish to men. When Elijah attempted to start a fire by first pouring water on the wood, he must have drawn ridicule from his opponents. Noah, building a mammoth boat on dry ground, must surely have drawn taunts about his intelligence, or, rather, lack of intelligence. Jesus' proposal to furnish wine at a wedding feast by filling pots with mere water must have appeared quite ridiculous to the onlookers. But all these foolish and absurd looking acts were ordained of God. The Lord God Almighty, in His infinite wisdom, hath chosen the foolish things of the world to confound the wise. Who am I to question God's omniscience?

The Jews who were present on the day of Pentecost were just as perplexed as many are today. What does this mean? What is the interpretation of these events? That bold, always ready to act man, Simon Peter, stepped forth to answer their questions. Today, the task of arriving at an answer must befall God's minister. May God's Spirit speak to your heart and mine as we attempt to answer this age-old question, "What Meaneth This?"

My remaining remarks are based on an outline from the excellent book *Pillars of Pentecost* by Charles W. Conn. Let us notice, first of all, what Pentecost did not mean.

It did not mean SALVATION or the NEW BIRTH. Some would say that these disciples were simply converted; that prior to this they had been a group of sinners, and Pentecost simply brought about a conversion experience. But how could this be? Is there any person who could live for three years in intimate communion with Christ, having obeyed God's will, and having received power to heal the sick and cast out devils, and not be a converted, born-again Christian? Jesus had said in Luke 10:20: "Rejoice, because your names are written in heaven." Surely, they were saved even when Christ lived on the earth. Had He not also prayed: "... They are not of the world, even as I am not of the world" (John 17:16)? No, Pentecost was not the bestowing of the New Birth or Salvation.

It did not mean SANCTIFICATION. Christ's prayer in John 17 was for their sanctification. "That they all may be one; as thou, Father, art in me, and I in thee, that they also may be one in us." Was this prayer answered before the outpouring of the Holy Ghost? Certainly so! "And when the day of Pentecost was fully come, they were all with one accord" (Acts 2:1). This marvelous oneness came sometime before the Holy Ghost came. Christian love and purity was already a part of their experience before the outpouring of the Holy Ghost.

Now what does the Holy Ghost fullness mean? Let us discuss several aspects of His coming.

He brought a tremendous exaltation and JOY. To the onlookers on the day of Pentecost, it seemed like a great stir of fanatics or enthusiasts. But these people could not imagine what was taking place in the hearts of these baptized believers. We sing a song sometimes that says, "It was joy, unspeakable and full of glory." Acts 13:52 says, "And the disciples were filled with joy, and with the Holy Ghost." What a contrast there is to worldly thrills and excitements: "For the kingdom of God is not meat and drink; but righteousness and peace, and joy in the Holy Ghost" (Romans 14:17).

Yet this blessing is more than joy. Beyond anything I, or any other person could express, the Holy Ghost baptism is POWER. "But ye shall receive power, after that the Holy Ghost is come upon you" (Acts 1:8). This power for service: power to proclaim the gospel, overcome evil, and to obey the will of God. This was the power that Paul and Silas manifested when they were so empowered that they could "turn the world upside down." This same kind of inner power of the Holy Ghost is that which "maketh... his ministers a flame of fire" (Hebrews 1:7). This is the power that Christianity needs today in order that we can go forth, endued with power from on high, that we might shake the world for God.

This blessing brought with it a TEACHER. There were times in Bible days, as well as the day in which we are living, that man needs something besides degrees, or diplomas, or learning based purely on a materialistic and secularistic foundation. Man needs a divine, a heavenly wisdom; a wisdom above and outside of himself. "For the Holy Ghost shall teach you in the same hour what ye ought to say" (Luke 12:12). Men and women who have the Baptism of the Holy Ghost have access to a knowledge and spiritual enlightenment that this world is not aware of. This teacher can equip the child of God so that he can "be ready always to give an answer to every man that asketh you a reason of the hope that is in you with meekness and fear" (I Peter 3:15).

Oh, thank God, the reception of the Holy Ghost meant that believers could receive a revealer of mysteries. "We speak, not in the words which man's wisdom teacheth, but which the Holy Ghost teacheth; comparing spiritual things with spiritual" (I Cor. 2:13). Further, "But the Comforter, which is the Holy Ghost, whom the Father will send in my name, he shall teach you all things, and bring all things to your remembrance, whatsoever I have said unto you" (John 14:26). Many times the saint of God may fall to his knees perplexed, seeking God for understanding, and then this heavenly Teacher floods the soul, illuminates the heart, and heavenly wisdom provides the answer.

This Pentecostal blessing did more – it provided a COMFORTER. Christianity never promises to any man a life of complete freedom from suffering and sorrow. Those who preach such a gospel do not find the basis for it in the Bible. But Christianity does promise that with the suffering God will provide a Comforter. "And I will pray the Father, and he shall give you another Comforter, that he may abide with you forever" (John 14:16). Christ had been the Comforter to these men and women before Pentecost. But it became necessary that He leave them; but comfortless, He said, I will not leave you. Born again believer, what a privilege you have today in your times of infirmities. The Scripture says that "Likewise the Spirit also helpeth our infirmities: for we know not what we should pray for as we ought: but the Spirit itself maketh intercession for us with groanings which cannot be uttered" (Romans 8:26). If you have never experienced the Holy Ghost as a Comforter, a Companion, One who walks along side you and strengthens you, you have missed one of the greatest Christian privileges.

But He is more. He is a SEALER. "Who hath also sealed us, and given the earnest of the Spirit in our hearts" (2 Cor. 1:22). As a notary uses his seal to impress his documents, the Holy Ghost deeply impresses us with His truth and likeness. The earnest of the Spirit is henceforward imbedded deeply in our heart. We are stamped as the property of our Savior.

I would that time would permit me to unfold more of these glorious truths about Pentecost. But even then, the full reply to "What Meaneth This?" could only be answered in eternity. I would that I could impress upon each Christian, each individual, the importance of receiving the Holy Spirit in His fullness. As vital as the "breath of God" was to Adam, so is the Holy Ghost vital to the church and you. May God grant the desire for this blessing to every heart.

7

The Need of the Hour

*B*e patient therefore, brethren, unto the coming of the Lord. Behold, the husbandman waiteth for the precious fruit of the earth, and hath long patience for it, until he receive the early latter rain. (James 5:7).

What is the need of this hour, of this day, of this age, in the light of what we know about the conditions of the world? For instance, we know that the world is standing closer to nuclear destruction than it ever has. Several years ago I read where certain atomic scientists moved the hands on a clock, pictured on the front of a bulletin, to just a few minutes before midnight. This signified, of course, their opinion that man was nearer an all-out nuclear war than ever before.

One poet described his anxiety and concern by reminiscing about the dropping of nuclear bombs at Christmas Island, Bikini, and in Nevada. And then in vivid and picturesque symbolism, he described a scientist in a breath-taking countdown to destruction. Then, in his imagination, he sees Gabriel in heaven, with trumpet to lips, as God also counts. The whole world, with bated breaths waits. Will God soon be saying "zero"? One does not have to be a poet, or a scholar, or a scientist to recognize the urgency of this hour in which we live.

Everywhere man looks – spiritually, morally, economically, politically, militarily – the world is in trouble. Someone has said that we Americans are being treated to a "ringside seat at the Day of Judgment." Man has tried every conceivable plan to solve the ills of society, but without avail. In the light of the many terrifying statistics that tell of crime and sin, what chance do we have?

Some professing Christians have even become discouraged. But the man of God recognizes that there is only one cure, one solution, to the troubles that confront us: and that is God's program of spiritual renovation of the hearts of man. The man of the world who is sober in his analysis of the world situation recognizes that sin is great, but the child of God stands firmly on the promises of His Word: "But where sin abounded, grace did much more abound." The cure for the sores of sin is an application of God's salve of grace and power. In other words, a revival of spiritual power is the need of the hour.

Friend, it seems to many of God's people that as we draw near to the end of this age, there seems to be an intensification of the work of the Holy Spirit. God seems to be calling out a people for His name and to be preparing them for His soon return to this earth.

There does seem to be a falling away; this is consistent with the state of affairs in the last days. There is a grave apostasy from the faith. But there also seems to be a hungering for the Spirit of God in the hearts of many believers. Many people from all faiths and denominations seem to possess a sense of need and a desire for a deeper experience with God. Even in our city I have heard of groups of people, from many denominations and stations in life, who are meeting together in prayer and fellowship groups, seeking more of God's blessings upon their lives. One leader in my church has made this statement: "The Holy Spirit has leaped out of its humble Pentecostal setting, over denominational barriers, and is overriding plan and program, ritual and ceremony, to satisfy longing hearts."

Someone might ask, "Is there a firm Biblical basis for believing in a latter day outpouring of the Spirit?" There certainly is! Those wonderful prophetic words of the prophet Joel that "I will pour out of my spirit upon all flesh" is being fulfilled in this generation. Those wonderful promises in the New Testament, given during the early days of the church, are not mere pages in the Book which served to inspire the early Christians, but only make us heart-sore because they are not available to us today. That wonderful, divine power that was bestowed upon the early church must not be looked upon as a once-for-all blessing, never to be received again. God did not bestow upon those early Christians divine power for service and encouragement for daily living, and then decide to withhold it from subsequent generations.

We believe the Christian may yet sing, "Every promise in the book is mine" and mean it. Christ commissioned the church to make believers in all the world and He gave the Spirit as the Source of power. He left to the church the challenge and privilege of praying for the sick, with the understanding that they should recover. He challenged men to preach His Word and to see transformed lives. He sent His disciples into a world (and still sends them) that is tormented by demonic powers, and told them to challenge the powers of evil, and that in the process the gates of hell would not prevail against them.

Now, with what power can you and I, as Christians, fulfill these commands to challenge, change, and convert men?

There is one simple answer: it will take the same source of power for us as it did for the Son of God. The writer in Luke quotes Christ as saying: "The Spirit of the Lord is upon me, because he hath anointed me to preach the gospel to the poor; he hath sent me to heal the brokenhearted, to preach deliverance to the captives, and recovering of sight to the blind, to set at liberty them that are bruised, to preach the acceptable year of the Lord" (Luke 4:18, 19). What was it that empowered Christ to so minister? The Spirit of the Lord.

If this world is to be transformed; if hearts are to be changed; if spirits of men are to be melted and molded; if Christians are to live victorious lives, we must have a renewal of fellowship with the Spirit of God. God has not left His church defenseless against the enemy. God has not abandoned Christians to a life of constant defeat. Rather, He promised in the last day that He would "pour out of His Spirit." Knowing that the return of Christ is soon, this is the day that believers should arise and appropriate the power which is provided through the Baptism with the Holy Spirit.

In a day of spiritual weakness, timidity and fear, once again men should echo the words of the prophet Zechariah: "Not by might, nor by power, but by my Spirit, saith the Lord." With the powerful array of enemy against the children of God, we can recognize that our means of dealing with Satan is not to return earthly force with earthly force. When the entire realm of Egypt sought to destroy the man, Moses, God was with His chosen one through the agency of the Spirit. When the prophet Elijah was being pursued by King Ahab, his wife Jezebel, the prophets of Baal, and apparently, the Israelite nation as well, it was then that God, through the agency of the Spirit, performed a great work of deliverance.

The whole world seemed to be against our Saviour Jesus Christ. They reviled Him; they unjustly tried Him, condemned Him, and crucified Him. But He remained victorious through every trial because the "Spirit of the Lord was upon Him."

The answer to the fire of the Atom bomb; the answer to the fire of sin that burns within the hearts of unrepentant sinners – the answer to these, I say, is the fire of the Holy Spirit. And this is precisely what Jesus promised to His followers. At least four times the Gospels repeat His prophetic promise: "... he shall baptize you with the Holy Ghost, and with fire" (Matthew 3:11); "... he shall baptize you with the Holy Ghost" (Mark 1:8); "... he shall baptize you with the Holy Ghost and with fire" (Luke 3:16); "... the same is he which baptizeth with the Holy Ghost" (John 1:33). These were prophetic announcements of things which were to be bestowed. Truly, the answer to the problem of this day is an outpouring of the fire of God.

The first thing we must do to gain this favor of God is to come to Him in faith and confidence. The apostle John had this to say: "And this is the confidence that we have in him, that, if we ask anything according to his will, he heareth us: And if we know that he hear us, whatsoever we ask, we know that we have the petitions that we desired of him" (I John 5:14, 15). Every Christian, every true believer, should familiarize himself and herself with the promises of God, so that we can recognize the bounty of God's goodness in these days. The failure of so many Christians is simply the failure to receive what God has promised. He has promised to "supply our needs" and yet we fail to believe God for this promise.

The second need of the hour is for Christian men and women to more fully consecrate themselves to Him.

Someone said to me not long ago, "Reverend, if every Christian would just get real close to the Lord we would see great revivals." I heartily disagree. It is not a matter of every Christian really consecrating himself to God; but, rather, there is a need of a "few" dedicated, consecrated, believing men and women who will really pray and fulfill the commands of God. When this happens, then revival fires will burn, lost souls will be saved, and the world will see Jesus.

8

Prayer

We want to take a limited but careful look at the matter of prayer as it relates to the subject of healing. Prayer has been called "the mightiest force in the universe." And likely it is. To "pray" is to "wish, to ask, to make a request, to desire, to call to one's aid." These are the kinds of elements that are often found in prayer.

First of all, the very fact that we pray to Someone designates the fact that we believe that One is abundantly able to do something about our requests. Psalm 65:2 indicates just exactly this: "O thou that hearest prayer, unto thee shall all flesh come..."

Oftentimes we hear Christians referring to God as a "prayer answering God." This is an indication that we believe that God can and does answer our requests and petitions; and not only does He consistently do so, but this fact has become synonymous with His nature, so that we constantly and consistently call Him the "prayer answering God." That is His name.

And even though the Bible may not indicate that answering prayer is specifically the nature of God; it certainly does flow from God's divine character and attributes. God's mercy, God's holiness, God's righteousness, these attributes of God are unchanging. Malachi 3:6 says, "I am the Lord,

I change not." Hebrews 13:8 says, "Jesus Christ the same yesterday, and today, and forever." And this God hears the prayers of "all flesh." Jew and Gentile, rich and poor, whoever it is that calls upon His name – He will hear them.

There has been no dispensation in which His divine grace has not permitted answers to prayer. Whether with Enoch, who walked with God and was taken to heaven prior to physical death, or with Abraham, who received the miracle of a longed-for child, God answered prayer. In all ages and dispensations: antediluvian (before the flood), after the flood, during the reign of the kings and the prophets, God answered prayer. During the sojourn of Christ on the earth, and the period after His resurrection, and through the continuing centuries following the completion of the canon of the Holy Scripture – God continued to answer prayer.

It is the very nature of God to answer prayer, even for those who are unworthy. While those of us who are ministers and teachers oftentimes limit answers to prayer to the saved; that is probably not consistent with the over-all Scriptural interpretation. Dr. H. A. Ironside, in his book, "Praying in the Holy Spirit," deals with, and gives evidence that even the unsaved have been recipients of God's miraculous power in the answering of prayers. The norm for Christians who are asking God for blessings, however, is to confess sin to God. Psalm 66:18 says, "If I regard iniquity in my heart, the Lord will not hear me."

Why should we pray? Well, one does not even need to answer that question; because men just naturally pray. Since the Bible says of Seth, in the early part of the recorded history of mankind, when "men began to call upon the name of the Lord" (Genesis 4:26), men have spontaneously called to God in their moments of need. There is a consistent pattern of calling out to God in moments of need: whether it was Jacob wrestling in prayer "unto the breaking of the day"; or Moses who "fell down before the Lord forty days and forty nights" in prayer; or David who "fasted and went in, and lay all night upon the earth" in prayer; or Elijah casting himself down upon the earth and putting his face between his knees in prayer; or Jesus who often arose "a great while before day" for prayer, and, on one occasion, "continued all night in prayer." Men have always spontaneously cried out to God in their moments of trial and times of trouble.

Men can reject God, and even deny there is a God, but let them get into trouble and the hardest heart, the most firm adamantine will soften. It has been said that even the atheist in the foxhole, when the bullets are flying and the bombs are bursting, will call upon the name of the Lord.

On one occasion I was riding with a funeral director in his car to attend the completion of a funeral service at the cemetery. He told me of an incident that took place the day before. A family lost a loved one; and, in this case, they were all professing atheists. The family requested that the director arrange a small memorial service at the graveside, at which there would be the recitation of some appropriate poetry and the like – but absolutely no Scripture or the mention of the name of God. He recounted to me the events of the ceremony. When it was concluded, one member of the family threw himself across the casket and cried aloud, "O God, O God."

Yes friend, men can intellectually and emotionally deny God, but when the moments of stress come, that heart-felt need and disposition to call upon a higher power, will gush forth like a torrent. There is a natural, native tendency for man to pray; hidden somewhere, yet even lurking beneath the doubts of agnosticism and atheism, there is a will-spring of hope and need and desire, placed there by God, that will break forth through the calloused souls of men and women. There are some things in life that men and women must, on occasion do, and one of those is to pray.

This short discourse makes no claim to being in complete detail about this subject; we shall leave a great deal more unsaid than we are saying; therefore we shall only hit the high spots. We are trying to relate our discussion specifically to the matter of healing. But the next question that arises is: "What should we pray for?"

Well, the answer, from the viewpoint of the Scriptures, is simply this: "Pray for anything and everything!" Somebody has said, "That anything you have a right to want, you have a right to ask for." Mark 11:23, 24 is a good Scriptural basis for this important question. It reads, "For verily I say unto you, That whosoever shall say unto this mountain, Be Thou removed, and be thou cast into the sea; and shall not doubt in his heart, but shall believe that those things which he saith shall come to pass; he shall have whatsoever he saith. Therefore I say unto you, What things so ever ye desire, when ye pray, believe that ye receive them, and ye shall have them."

Jesus said "Whatsoever" ye shall ask. Now whatsoever means anything and everything that is legitimate and good. The truth is that God offers an unlimited invitation to pray for the desires of the heart. It is true, then, that God encourages us not only to pray for the needs, but also for the wants.

John 15:7 says, "If ye abide in me, and my words abide in you, ye shall ask what ye will, and it shall be done unto you." What should I pray for? Jesus says, "What ye will." There is a vast amount of territory covered by that statement. Psalm 37:4 says, "Delight thyself also in the Lord; and he shall give thee the desires of thine heart."

Now someone is saying, are you telling us that the Bible says I can have whatever I need and desire and ask for? The answer is potentially, yes. God says to ask for it; therefore it is potentially available.

We shall discuss some of the reasons people do not get their prayers answered; but God has established no initial limitations on our ability and right to ask for whatever we need and desire. Therefore we must assume that the answer to our prayer request is potentially and possibly obtainable.

Someone has said, "To pray about everything, in submission to God's will, would be both more human and more Christian than a scrupulous limitation of our prayers to what we might think permissible subjects of petition." Amen!

Is it not strange how illogical Christians think sometimes? We lead ourselves to believe that God is only interested in the great and large problems and needs of life. Therefore we bypass the smaller, lesser needs with our prayers.

I remember as a young man hearing an old saint testify to calling upon God to heal his sick mule: my unbelieving response was – how nonsensical! Later, I heard another saint testify to asking God to repair the washing machine. Again, I thought, how foolish! But, in both cases, the petitioners testified to the miraculous intervention of God, during which the mule was restored to health, and the washing machine, instantly, began to run.

But the foolish person is the one who limits and negates the power of God. Nowhere does God belittle His children for asking for the fulfillment of any need, be it in the realm of the vegetable, animal and mineral portions of His earthly realm. As a matter of fact, ample evidence is available in the Bible for all manner of miracles: from the filling of an oil barrel to a miraculous draught of fish; from the swimming of an inert piece of an ax head to the infusion of human vocabulary into the mouth of a donkey.

Well, someone is thinking, you mean I can pray for anything I want? The answer is, "yes." Ask for anything you "want" that is in conformity to the will of God. Now, not to cast cold water on the subject; but some people do need to get their **wanters** fixed so that they will be in conformity to the will of God. But anything that God wants you to have, you have a right to want and to pray for.

Philippians 4:6 says, "Be careful for nothing but in everything by prayer and supplication with thanksgiving let your requests be made known unto God. And the peace of God, which passeth all understanding, shall keep your hearts and minds through Christ Jesus." Again, in EVERYTHING, let your requests be made known to God.

The cure for anxiety is to bombard the battlements of glory with our requests. God has placed before us the unlimited resources of heaven; and heaven encourages us to come to Him "in everything by prayer and supplication with thanksgiving." We are, thus, to let our requests be made known.

How many folk have sung the old gospel song without really knowing what they were singing?

> *"What a Friend we have in Jesus,*
> *All our sins and griefs to bear!*

What a privilege to carry
EVERYTHING to God in prayer.
"O, what a peace we often forfeit,
O, what needless pain we bear,
All because we do not carry
EVERYTHING to God in prayer!

Now, the truth is, God is exhorting His people to pray. Prayer is not some optional attachment to our Christian vehicle. God says, "My house shall be called the house of prayer." And he spoke a parable on one occasion to this effect: "... that men ought always to pray, and not to faint" (Luke 18:1). And the apostle Paul exhorted us to "Pray without ceasing" (I Thessalonians 5:17). And the Old Testament prophet Samuel said, "Moreover as for me, God forbid that I should sin against the Lord in ceasing to pray for you..." (I Samuel 12:23).

What a beautiful study in the Bible just to find out who and what we are to pray for. We are to pray for all men, for kings, for those in authority, for the saints, for our enemies, for wants, for needs, for physical healing and, in fact, we are just to pray for everything. That leaves the question of what we should pray for an open-ended matter.

It is a strange thing to me, what with all the subject matter available in the Bible on the matter of prayer – that our faith friends should say, "all you need is faith." Friend, **faith is not even a subject for discussion until you have prayed about it.** There is an old song that says, "Have you prayed about it yet." I hardly think that one needs to do anything until prayer has been engaged in.

II Chronicles 7:14 says, "If my people, which are called by my name, shall humble themselves, and pray, and seek my face, and turn from their wicked ways; then will I hear from heaven, and will forgive their sin, and will heal their land." Oh, this over-emphasis on faith that men are entering into. NO wonder that holiness and purity and righteousness have become nonentities before this causal superficial, humanistic emphasis that says, "Just you have faith."

Prayer is that heavenly detergent that cleanses the soul; prayer is the heavenly anointing that prepares the heart; prayer is the hand that plugs into the heavenly switchboard so that we can get in tune with God's will, so that we can get on the heavenly vibrations so that we can move in cadence with God. Jesus prayed at the tomb of Lazarus and said, "Father, I thank thee that thou hast heard me. And I knew that thou hearest me always..." (John 11:41, 42).

Now, precisely, why do we pray? Well, a lot of folk have a misconception of the reasons for prayer. Some believe that one prays in order to give God information. If we really think we pray in order to give God information, we have a shallow understanding of the divine omniscience. God is not dependent upon men for knowledge or information. John 2:24, 25 said, "Jesus did not commit himself unto them, because he know all men. And needed not that any should testify of man: for he knew what was in man."

And the powerful truth of the matter is clearly made known in Hebrews 4:13, "Neither is there any creature that is not manifest in his sight: but all things are naked and opened unto the eyes of him with whom we have to do." And if these Scriptures are not clear enough, Jesus made it plain in Matthew 6:8: "... for your Father knoweth what things ye have need of, before ye ask him." A number of Scriptures we have given make it plain that we are to confess and make known our needs to God; but the reason is not so that we can impart wisdom and knowledge to the infinite mind of this universe, God.

Another reason we do not pray is to change the mind of God. How often I have made this mistake; I have pleaded uncontrollably, with the thought in mind that I must get God over on my side. I have secretly thought that perhaps I could persuade God to agree with me. As someone has said, "to think that we can persuade God to side with us on a given proposition is a childish delusion."

Our problem is, of course, we constantly attempt to think of God on human terms. This is the fallacious, simplistic thinking of so many folk today. Acts 15:18 says, "Known unto God are all his works from the beginning of the world." Now, to me, this is not some fatalistic, predestination, that makes null and void the free will of man. But it is a declaration that God has always, and will always work according to His immutable, unchanging character.

His attitudes will always favor holiness, righteousness, good, the wise and the like. And His attitudes will always be against sin, unrighteousness, evil, and the like. We can rest assured of one thing: God will deal with man according to man's just deserts. But God does not change. "For I am the Lord, I change not" (Malachi 3:6).

Now the question often arises, "But the Bible seems to indicate that God does change His attitude; does He not?" It is not our purpose to enter into this discussion; but suffice it to say that several answers are possible.

First, the Bible may describe a change in God's attitude in order to accommodate our human language and understanding. There are things about God and His acts that are foreign to our mortal understanding.

Second, God often times makes promises conditionally. And when something takes place on the part of man, for instance repentance, then God is freed to change His method and mode of operation toward that person. Thus God can change – not His character or basic attitudes; but He can change the manner in which He deals with that man. In any case, any essential change in the matter of prayer is on the part of man.

Somewhat in the same connection as the desire to change God's mind, is the desire to compel a reluctant God. But Jesus, in Matthew 23:27, makes God's attitude clear on this point: "How often would I... and ye would not." Billheimer said, "Who know's how much God would do for His servants if He dared."

Is God reluctant? Not according to Isaiah. "And it shall come to pass, that before they call, I will answer; and while they are yet speaking, I will hear" (Isaiah 65:24). Now while Luke 18, the parable of the judge and the widow, and Luke 11, the story of the man who needed bread, do, of necessity, teach that we should engage in importunate prayer (continuous prayer); they do not in fact teach us that God is reluctant. I Peter 3:12, "For the eyes of the Lord are over the righteous, and his ears are open unto their prayers: but the face of the Lord is against them that do evil."

Now, then, why do we pray? My study of prayer reveals one basic reason why we pray; there are, of course, several points that tie in with this one. But, basically, we pray in order to prepare a person and his circumstances to receive the answer. I Chronicles 7:14 says, "If my people, which are called by my name, shall humble themselves, and pray, and seek my face, and turn from their wicked ways; then will I hear from heaven, and will forgive their sin, and will heal their land." We pray in order to get our hearts prepared and made ready, so that God can give us an answer to our prayer.

I hear it often said by our faith friends: "Pray one time and cease praying. Any praying beyond that shows a lack of faith." This is not a new teaching, but it is unscriptural and simplistic. The problem is they do not understand what prayer is all about. Prayer and faith are not necessarily synonymous terms. One often wonders where some of these new teachings come from.

Now, while I believe that God could, and has, on occasion, given a positive assurance with the first prayer that some people have prayed; this is surely not the general manner in with God works. The Scriptures are so numerous that refute this idea of praying only one time, that one is amazed that the advocates of this pray one time, and praying beyond that shows lack of faith, have not seen them. Let us look at several of them.

In the story found in Exodus chapter 17 we have Moses standing on the top of a hill facing a battle between the Amalekites and the Israelites. As long as Moses held his hands up, the battle went in favor of the Israelites; when his hands fell, the Amalekites began to win. While prayer is not explicitly mentioned, there is no reason that we should believe that Moses did not engage in fervent prayer. A continuous, fervent intercessory prayer vigil brought the victory.

I think also of Daniel who prayed and fasted for three weeks before God brought the answer. And think of Jesus Himself who prayed on at least three occasions, repeating the same prayer, concerning the matter of the cross. No, this idea of pray one time, and then cease praying, because any prayers offered beyond that show a lack of faith, are totally inconsistent with a balanced view of Scripture. The problem with this kind of thinking that is being generated in so many places today is this: People are simply grasping at something that sounds good without determining its logical consequences, and without comparing Scripture with Scripture.

No, prayer is for more purposes than just a simple exercise of faith. Again, this solution is too simplistic; it fails to deal with the whole counsel of God. While everything we obtain is gotten, essentially, by faith; it is also true that faith operates within an environment that includes such elements as prayer, certain conditions, the will of God and other important elements.

We also pray in order to commune with God. Now in an age that the emphasis is becoming humanistic, even among evangelical Christians; the Biblical emphasis is still on God. When I approach God, am I really concerned about glorifying god, or am I concerned just with my physical wellbeing? The primary purpose of the creation of man is still: "to God be the glory…" Some of the self-centered, man-centered theology has departed a great distance from this truth.

We also pray in order to ascertain the will of God. We have pointed out that the will of God is always whatever is good and right; but we, as mortal human beings, do not always know what is good and right and best in every situation. Life is not that simple; can we not understand that? God wants the best for us; that is the best from His vantage point, not ours.

While you and I might think that healing, right at that moment is the best for us; God, from the perspective of heaven may know better – He may know some things, some consequences of that action that we are unaware of. To assume that one always knows the will of God, perfectly, in every situation is, as one writer said it, "to be wise above what is written."

Bible characters often "enquired of the Lord." What about David? David was not sure until his child died exactly what the will of God was in this particular situation. What will our faith teachers do with this verse, since they tend to take every Scripture literally? Here it is: "And he (David) said, While the child was yet alive, I fasted and wept: for I said, Who can tell whether God will be gracious to me, that the child may live?" (II Samuel 12:22). What David is saying is this: I simply did not know what the will of God was in this particular situation, until God chose to take the child in death.

What about Paul? He prayed not once, but three times, seeking to rid himself of a thorn in the flesh. And until God directly illuminated his thinking, then, and then only, did Paul recognize the will of God. God, Himself, finally had to tell Paul that, "My grace is sufficient for thee" (I Corinthians 12:7-9).

And whatever the understanding of the situation might have been, even Jesus prayed, "Father, if thou be willing, remove this cup from me: nevertheless not my will, but thine, be done" (Luke 22:42). Do you not see it friend; it is too simplistic to say that God, at this moment, wills thus and so. Prayer is a means of determining the exact nature of God's will. To attempt to exercise faith without first determining the precise, exact will of God may be an exercise in futility.

A. W. Tozer railed quite effectively against these "one prayer" individuals. He disputed the claim of these folk who

reason that if we believe the first time we pray, then we have
the answer; and a second prayer betrays the unbelief of the
first: therefore, let there be no second prayer. Tozer says
there are three things wrong with this teaching.

One, "it ignores a large body of Scripture. Two, "it rarely
works in practice, even for the saintliest soul." Three, "if
persisted in, it robs the praying man of two of his mightiest
weapons in his warfare with the flesh and the devil:
intercession and petition."

He goes on to say that "Had David subscribed to the
one prayer creed he could have reduced his psalms to
about one-third their present length. Elijah would not have
prayed seven times for rain (and incidentally, there would
have been no rain, either), our Lord would not have prayed
the third time 'saying the same words,' nor would Paul have
'besought the Lord thrice' for the removal of his thorn.

"In fact, if this teaching were true, much wonderful
Biblical narrative would have to be rewritten, for the
Bible has much to say about continued and persistent
prayer." Tozer goes on to say that "the devil has no fear of
such Christians. He has already won over them, and his
technique has been false logic."

Watchman Nee, with whom I do not always agree, says
much the same thing. He says, "Such prayer (persistent
prayer) does not conflict with that in Mark 11. Mark tells us
that we ought to pray till we are given faith; here (Luke 18:1)
we are told that we ought to pray always and not to faint.

The old-timers said to pray until "You pray through."
May the Lord help some of us newcomers to grasp some of
those old tried and true truths. "Praying through" means
you have the answer; you have arrived at the mind and
will of God in a matter. It is the height of spiritual pride to

assume that one knows that is best in a given situation without consulting God.

We pray in order to obtain God's help. Without divine enablement we are unable to battle the forces of life. Ephesians 6:12 says, "For we wrestle not against flesh and blood, but against principalities, against powers, against the rulers of the darkness of this world, against spiritual wickedness in high places."

We pray in order to cooperate with God. Most people who have studied the matter of prayer could probably agree on one statement; "God does nothing except in answer to prayer." God created man with "spirit and soul and body," therefore He made man to live in a universe that is spiritual, intellectual, and physical. Therefore, the three keys that unlock the resources of this universe are prayer, thought, and work. We definitely need all three in our Christian walk.

Prayer is the key to the definite resources of God's spiritual supply. Prayer does not change God's reluctance; it does not change the divine purpose or intention – these were and are unchangeable. But prayer does release God's power and permits Him to work in a given situation. Until the heart of man is conditioned and prepared and made ready by prayer, God is not free to work.

Simply stated: one of the laws by which God has limited Himself is the law of prayer. But the prayers of the child of God prepare the man and release God's power so that He can begin to work. When man prays and conditions himself, then all of heaven is free to attack the forces of evil or whatever stands in the way of the perfect will of God being done.

There is an important point we must not overlook. The question might be asked, "Well, if we have prayed through, if we have ascertained the mind and will of God – what next?" The answer is, "Begin praising God." This is the point where one might start praying in unbelief and doubt if he or she is not careful. One overcomes this by praising. Billheimer says, "Satan is allergic to praise, so where there is massive, triumphant praise, Satan is paralyzed, bound, and banished." Praise, friend, is a heavenly detergent that will flush out the demonic dregs and dirt; and will permit the free-flow of divine glory.

Praise is so important that an entire order of beings in heaven spend their time in praising (Revelation 4:8). God gave to King David such an important revelation of praise that, following the heavenly pattern, he set aside on earth a dedicated army of four thousand Levites whose sole occupation was to praise the Lord (I Chronicles 23:5). Is praise any less important to the child of God today? Surely not!

The important question may still arise, "Why, when I pray for physical healing, does not God always answer my prayer?" Let us look at some of the answers; we shall consider these in a limited fashion, inasmuch as we shall deal more completely with this subject under another section. But let us notice several vital facts.

Let us look at I John 5:14, 15: "And this is the confidence that we have in him, that, if we ask anything according to his will, he heareth us: And if we know that he hear us, whatsoever we ask, we know that we have the petitions that we desired of him" These verses indicate that if we ask anything, that is in prayer, from God, that is according to His will, He will hear us. A careful study of the matter of unanswered prayer has brought me to one conclusion: I believe that, in the light of what we read in the

Bible, God does always answer prayer, or, at least, responds to the prayers of the individual child of God.

As someone has said, God answers prayer in three ways: He says, "Yes, or No, or Wait-a-while." I believe those are three valid responses that God gives to prayer. Does He ever say No? Yes He does: if we ask "amiss" (James said, "Ye ask, and receive not, because ye ask amiss, that ye may consume it upon your own lusts" (James 4:3). Or if we remain outside the conditions (have sin, wrong motives and the like), God will reject our request.

A Scriptural example is the "thorn in the flesh" of Paul. Its removal was rejected lest he be lifted up with spiritual pride and "fall into the condemnation of the devil" (I Timothy 3:6). If Paul, who was ushered into the Trinitarian council of God and was given revelatory truths beyond anything we could imagine, stood in danger of being "exalted above measure through the abundance of the revelations: lest (he) should be exalted above measure" (II Corinthians 12:7); how could we be foolish enough to imagine that God would not have to deal with us because of the same or similar reasons, and thus be forced sometimes to say "no!"?

To imagine that some puny, frail, arrogant, young spiritual whippersnapper could stride pridefully into the presence of the Almighty and wrest from God whatever he or she wanted on the basis of their "have faith, confess it, it is done" formula, defies a thinking man's imagination.

Being a human father or mother should make it easy to understand why sometimes God must say a resounding "no"! The truth is that the Bible and experience reveal that God, more often than not, has to say no. Those who deny that statement have not been keeping score; they have only counted the wins, and they have failed to count the losses.

And then, sometimes, God says "yes." We must believe that when men and women pray, and have faith, and meet the conditions, and then act in accordance to the perfect will of God; that in such a case God will say "yes"! We must believe that, without exception, God always wants to say yes – if the thing requested in prayer conforms to the best interests of all the parties involved and if all the Biblical conditions have been met.

And one final truth which seems to me to help our understanding of the matter of apparently unanswered prayer: this fits into the category of "wait awhile." This final solution is quite satisfactory in answering some of the problems that do not easily fit into the categories of yes or no.

Follow this reasoning: If a man is desperately sick and comes to God in prayer and asks for healing from his sickness – does God or does God not want to heal that sickness? The answer, in light of everything we have said, and in light of everything that we seem to find in the Bible, is an unequivocal, Yes!

Consider the matter further. I John 3:8 says, "For this purpose the Son of God was manifested, that he might destroy the works of the devil." While it is a terribly false assumption that all sickness and sin, or the like, is always immediately caused by the devil or demons; it is indisputably true that at the instigation of Satan the first man and woman fell from righteousness, and the ensuing sin and evil that came into the world, with all their consequences, stemmed from that first act (Romans 5:12). Therefore, it is easily determined that Jesus sought to destroy all harmful and undesirable effects of that fall; thus Jesus seeks to eliminate and eradicate sickness. Who could deny that statement?

This all falls into the category of the absolute will of God. Now, if as we have proposed, God wants to grant that request to heal someone's sickness; but does not, because of one of the elements that we have mentioned (sin, pride, etc.); does that mean that God has not, or will not, answer that prayer? In other words have we exhausted all the possibilities?

The answer is a resounding No! I do not believe that I have ever seen this answer, but here it is. We mortal, finite human beings tend to overlook a crucial and important point: "God has all eternity to answer that prayer; and I am confident, somewhere, sometimes, in the ages of ages yet to come, that prayer will be finally answered: so that the good, which may not have been the best for the child of God, will ultimately be answered.

In a sense, it may be said that all prayer according to the will of God will be answered. Do we have any Scripture? Certainly. In some verses that are usually referred to the millennium we read: "Then the eyes of the blind shall be opened, and the ears of the deaf shall be unstopped. Then shall the lame man leap as a hart, and the tongue of the dumb sing..." (Isaiah 5:5, 6). And in Revelation 21:4 we read, "And God shall wipe away all tears from their eyes; and there shall be no more death, neither sorrow, nor crying, neither shall there be any more pain: for the former things are passed away."

The old saying goes, "God never gets in a hurry, but He never arrives too late." Joni Eareckson may not receive her healing this side of the pearly gates (I have and am still praying for it, however); but she shall leap as a hart in that new home. A blind Fanny Crosby never saw a choir director lift his baton and lead a massed choir in one of her beautiful hymns; but in heaven she shall see the heavenly choir sing redemption's song. The difference between God and man is this: GOD HAS ALL ETERNITY TO MAKE GOOD ON HIS PROMISES.

9

The Laws of God

In my way of thinking, one of the most important elements in understanding the subject of healing arises at this point – that is, the laws of God. First of all, let us look at a definition of the word "law." Webster's Dictionary defines law as: "...all the rules of conduct established and enforced by (an) authority." There are other definitions, but this will suffice for our purposes.

Laws are necessary; who would deny that? Sometimes we do not like them when they are at cross-purposes with what we want; but in the long run we would not deny their usefulness. Without laws this world would be utter chaos. Without the laws of nature, such as gravity, it would be impossible to live on this planet earth. Without the law of gravity everything would be floating in mid-air. We take it for granted that when we get out of bed, and plant our foot on the floor, that that foot is going to remain stationary there until we bring into play a higher law, the law of force.

Yes, the laws of nature are taken for granted; we seldom view the beneficial nature of these blessed laws. Also, without laws among the civil affairs of men, society would be virtually chaotic. Without so common a law as the placement of red lights, riding in an automobile would be more of a nightmare than it already is. True, men can break laws, but there is a penalty for doing so.

Now, just as there are laws in the natural and civil realms; there are also laws in the spiritual realm as well. A careful study of Scripture will reveal a series of laws that God established to govern mankind. For instance, God established a prohibition against the eating of fruit from a certain tree "which (was) in the midst of the garden" (Genesis 3:3). Conscience, the Torah (the first five books of the Old Testament), the Ten Commandments, and even in this dispensation, the "law of Christ" (Galatians 6:2), enumerate just a few "of the rules of conduct established and enforced by God."

God, of necessity, operates according to lawful standards. The laws of God arise out of the nature of God; not from some outside source. And I believe men could easily agree that God's laws are perfect, always just, and are dispensed with mercy. Could we not, then, agree on one salient point: since God believes in laws, establishes laws, and deals with men on the basis of law, would it not be proper to say that God Himself must also live by, and in a sense, obey the laws that He Himself has established?

In the recent fiasco in our nation concerning the former President Nixon, astute authorities on law said, "Even the President is not above the law." In a reverential sense, we could say that even God is not above His laws: especially since He ordained them.

A person could simply not believe that everything would be anything but absolutely chaos unless God made an orderly and lawful society to live in, both civilly and spiritually. God is the only Being in this universe who will be absolutely true to His nature; hence, God will be true to the laws He has established; that is, He will not waver in executing them, neither will he execute them except fairly and justly, as only God can do.

And a special word to those who think they have a special handle on truth, or faith, or inroads to special privileges from God, note this: God takes into consideration the good of all, not the special interests of some. Those hyper-spiritual, white hat, good-guys, who think they have a corner on the market with God's blessings, have miscalculated the kind of person that God is.

Now we come to an exceedingly interesting and important point. Please do not turn me off until you have heard me out. Sometime ago I was reading a book that was dealing with the problems that are in the world as they are related to the Person of God. Important points were raised about the "Problem of Evil?" And, why does God permit sin in the world?

When one, for instance, turns on the evening news and sees the starving youngsters in Biafra or Bangladesh, what kind of person is that who, dining on a T-bone steak, golden French fries, and a delicious tossed-salad, does not lay his fork aside and say, "But why does God allow that?"

I often wondered, out loud, why these folk who have hold of neat little formulas that say, "Have faith, confess it, it is yours"; why they do not call down a few shiploads of food to assuage the hunger of those bloated bellies? If prosperity is the simplistic, easily obtainable thing that some folk say that it is (and I believe in "Biblical" prosperity) – why is it that their little clichés, and pat prosperity formulas only work in affluent America and, obviously, do not work so well behind the Iron Curtain or in the stinking ghettos of India, or the hot, humid jungles of Africa? Now, some of my faith friends will say that is begging the issue; no, but it is stating the facts.

Doctrine cannot close its eyes to the facts; it must take them into consideration. Any person whose eyes are open and whose mind is not closed, knows that this world is full of sin, evil, despair, sickness and unrighteousness.

Now this book I was reading dealt with these kinds of problems. Then the author raised an important question, which went as follows: "If God is Almighty, why doesn't He do better?" That is a pretty big question; I am not sure anybody has ever completely found the answer. But, after all, a "mighty man" is someone whom you expect to succeed. Whether its war, or a ball game, or in a business transaction, in fact, whatever it might be, you expect a "mighty man" to come out on top. A "mighty man," neighbor, gets things done. You do not expect failure; you expect success.

The truth is, then, we have come to believe that a "mighty man" is going to overcome his adversaries and throw down his rivals. And not only that, but Christians speak about God in terms of not just being a "mighty" man; but from an "Almighty Man," one would expect certain and continual success; a constant and total defeat of his rivals; and this, always, all the time, and perfectly and completely.

But is this the case; is this what we see in the world? Obviously not! The billionaires, almost without exception, are pagans and non-Christians. Wars are on the increase; crime is raging like a wind-swept fire out of control; licentiousness and immorality are the order of the day; the moral fabric of even our American society is becoming rotten; and the unrighteous flaunt their permissive standards in the face of the righteous. And what Christian is there alive who cannot point to at least one professing Christian who has used him or her as a doormat to attain to his selfish, carnally motivated ends.

Now, I know I keep raising the question of this book without giving you the man's answer. But I suppose I wanted to spare you the shock, if that be possible. Again, the question: "If God is Almighty, why doesn't He do better?" And the shocking answer, which ties in with what we have been saying: The answer is simply that **He can't** – that is, **so long as He observes the limitations of the rules which He has set for Himself in the running of the world.**

Now I want to let that sink in. When I first read those words, I protested loudly, at least in my spirit. There was no way, at that moment, that I was about to accept the absurdity of that statement. My spirit rejected it; my intellect sought for a thousand and one arguments to refute it; my emotions poured coals of wrath upon the man who would even intimate such a thing.

You mean, Almighty God cannot do better? But friend, the truth is, God either can or He cannot; and if He is not doing better (that is erasing sin and evil every time they raise their ugly heads), then "why not?" And then I came to see the truth: "God cannot do better – so long as he observes the limitations of the rules which He has set for Himself in the running of the world."

I do not profess that I shall answer your questions; I have not answered all my questions. I waded through probably the finest evangelical mind of the twentieth century, C. S. Lewis's *The Problem of Pain*, and I still had unanswered questions. I tackled what I believe to be one of the finest works on the subject, *The Goodness of God,* by John W. Wenham, and still came up short. But let us look at the matter, particularly in regards to its relationship to the suffering of sickness.

Pardon the personal illustration, but I believe that it illustrates what we are about to say. I remember on one occasion facing a man concerning a problem. The man was my superior, and, as in the case of someone who has greater authority than someone else, he sat, as we say, "In the driver's seat." Now, not only was he in the driver's seat; but he was supremely in the driver's seat.

After several conversations, during which I considered he hedged, equivocated, and changed his opinions quite often, I became exasperated. In my not so humble manner, I finally blurted out my true feelings about his handling of the whole situation and I said, "You know, sir, it is great to be a player in a game, and to be able to make the rules of the game as you play it. There is no way you can lose." And he did not lose!

But this episode is precisely the erroneous idea we have about the Person of Almighty God. We believe He cannot lose (in a sense, He cannot). And we believe this because we also believe that God makes the rules as He goes along (if you do not believe in free-will), and, thus, God is always a winner.

The statements are false on both counts. First, God's absolute will, as we pointed out in the section on the will of God, is obviously not always done – hence the sin and evil in the world. And, secondly, God does not make the rules of the game as He goes along – like some dictatorial tyrant.

The laws, the rules of conduct, are indelibly ingrained in the nature of God and have been throughout all eternity. God is not some capricious, whimsical, spur-of-the-moment Being, who arbitrarily waves His hand and says that person will go to heaven and that one will go to hell. Absolutely not!

The question arises, "Could God immediately banish all the sin and evil and sickness and suffering from the world?" From a viewpoint of power, the answer is obviously, "Yes, He could." But there are other factors to be considered other than brute force.

Tyrants, dictators, Hitlers, Herods, harsh brutal men act like that. They smother freedom; they banish free choice. Like the communists they turn men into a mechanistic apparatus, into cold, sterile pawns, to be shoved about as they will. But that is not God.

When God created free-willed men, He did so with the knowledge that they could mar and destroy their lives; they could degrade everything that was pure and holy. And has not man done a superb job of wrecking God's creation?

But, on the other hand, would you, as a mother or father, rather have children or puppets? There should be no debate here. Who wants a cold, lifeless, will-less robot who cannot return love? Nobody! Having love means risking.

This is what Paul talked about in II Corinthians 5:14, 15: "For the love of Christ constraineth us; because we thus judge, that if one died for all, then were all dead: And that he died for all, that they which live should not henceforth live unto themselves, but unto him which died for them, and rose again." God simply wants a spontaneous, loving relationship from men.

Oh, God could put all the ducks in a row; He could nicely assemble His little creatures in an orderly fashion; He could manipulate them like marionettes on a string – but He would not have men, He would have robots: and robots cannot respond with love. It was in no way possible for God to make men human beings, with the power of choice, with all its consequences, without making it possible for evil and sin and suffering to exist in this cursed world.

In no way let our statements indicate that God is not in control in this world: He is. We know what ultimately the end is going to be (especially from the book of Revelation); we know that God has established a framework of history in which men exercise their free choices; we know that God can overrule sin and evil and suffering to His greater glory (Romans 8:28); we know that Satan cannot touch a Christian, unless God permits him to do so (Job 2:6). Yes, God is in control.

But God has established laws, and He will permit a person to jump off a building and perish (and even permit a Christian to fall off and die). And some of us who believe in healing should take notice at this point; God will permit you to overeat and violate the laws of nature and suffer the consequences of that violation of His natural laws. Christians are not immune from these natural laws.

It is foolhardiness and unintelligence to deliberately violate these laws of God and think one can get away with it, just because one is a Christian. Christians do have angels, and God does sometimes grant special mercies to His people, and we should pray for them, but **ordinarily** it "rains on the just and the unjust" and "he maketh his sun to rise on the evil and the good" (Matthew 5:45).

God gave dietary laws in the unenlightened ages, but He expects us to know better. Is not much of the sickness today the results of our rejection of the known laws of God? And in this present evil world Christians have to breathe the same polluted air the non-Christians breathes; we have to eat the same contaminated foods the non-Christians eats; we drink the same impure water the non-Christian drinks.

There is a definite correlation between our sins (indiscretions, mistakes – call them what you may) and our sicknesses. Isaiah 33:24 says, "None in the land shall say I am sick, for all that live there have their sins forgiven" (Moffatt). An eminent doctor said: "If people lived in a truly Christian way, half the diseases would drop off tomorrow morning, and we would rise up a new, superior race of human beings."

There is also the matter of the consequences of "corporate sins" which must be taken into consideration. In the Old Testament did not the children suffer the consequences of the sins of the fathers unto "the third and forth generations" (Exodus 2:5).

Now, to believe that God's will is being perfectly done in this world does not square with either experience, as we have pointed out, or with Scripture. Consistently, Scripture teaches us that the course of this world and age is dictated by the prince of the power of the air – Satan (Ephesians 2:2). "Wherein in time past ye walked according to the course of this world, according to the prince of the power of the air, the spirit that now worketh in the children of disobedience." Furthermore, "...we know that... the whole world (cosmos) lieth in wickedness" (I John 5:19). And we also know that Satan is the "god of this world" (II Corinthians 4:4).

This is the kind of world that God is permitting. While it is true, unquestionably, that the devil is "a defeated foe," it is just as true that God has not exercised His, God's, final and complete eradication of Satan's influence; the book of Revelation makes clear when that shall be.

Now let's reiterate what we have been saying. God is not limited in what He can or cannot do. God has "all-power"; therefore, without question, He has the strength to banish, override, overcome and defeat any enemy or force on earth. He is "all-wise"; therefore God has infinite wisdom and can out-smart anybody or anything – He is there waiting for the devil when the devil is setting up his trap. God is "all-knowing," therefore God has superior intelligence and can, conceivably, out-think anybody. And we could continue.

No, God is not limited in what He can or cannot do; but God limits Himself by the establishment of divine laws. The sovereign will of God cannot be thwarted or overcome by the will of man, or of an angel, or the devil himself. God has limited Himself.

This is what Jesus Christ, the Son of God, did in Philippians 2:7: "But made himself of no reputation and took upon him the form of a servant. And was made in the likeness of men." Jesus laid aside His divine prerogatives; He temporarily veiled Himself in the limitations of mortal flesh. When a greater purpose was to be gained; even Almighty God could condescend to reach such a low level.

It is quite unfortunate, at least as far as it leads men to form perverted doctrine, that some folk today fail to realize where they are living. Ephesians, chapter one, establishes the environment of the Christian life. The word "environment" means to "circle around." As Christians, we are not yet in heaven; we have not yet arrived.

Paul says that the Christian life is lived first, "in Christ." Second, our life is lived in fellowship with the saints (Ephesians 1:1). But, third, our lives are lived in Ephesus, that is, the world around us. We as Christians still live in a world dominated, for the most part, by the "god of this world," that is Satan. It is a world of evil, suffering, challenges, and tribulations.

Now, while the Christian has some marvelous promises that he or she can utilize, a certain basic truth must still remain. Paul says that while you as Christians are in Christ, and live in the fellowship of the saints, and even though you have been "sealed with that Holy Spirit of promise, Which is the earnest (the down payment) of our inheritance," these things are only "until the redemption of the purchased possession..." (Ephesians 1:13, 14).

In other words, the total redemption of our lives is not yet. We have to live in this world, with all its attendant evils and suffering, until the day of final redemption. Thank God, that does not mean that God has not failed to provide blessed promises and provisions on the way to glory – He has. But the total, final redemption is "not yet."

Another thing that we must remember is that God did not author this evil that is in the world. Romans 5:13 says, "Wherefore, as by one man sin entered into the world, and death by sin; and so death passed upon all men, for that all have sinned."

The Biblical story tells us that Satan was the culprit who introduced the temptation to sin into the world; and man bit his rotten apple. The person behind the sin of Adam and Eve was Satan. Isaiah 14:12-14 says, "How art thou fallen from heaven, O Lucifer, son of the morning! How art thou cut down to the ground, which didst weaken the nations! For thou hast said in thine heart, I will ascend into heaven. I will exalt my throne above the stars of God: I will sit also upon the mount of the congregations, in the sides of the north: I will ascend above the heights of the clouds: I will be like the most High."

Therefore, God is not responsible for sin and its consequences; the primary blame goes back to the

Devil, and the immediate cause can lie in several different directions – but, in no case, does God bear any responsibility.

What kind of logic leads a person to believe that he or she will only suffer if he or she, personally, breaks a law? I know of a young, bright minister whose life was recently snuffed out by a drunk, driving on the wrong side of the road. Where does anyone arrive at the conclusion that one is immune from the consequences of the laws of God?; And, unfortunately, the innocent often suffer with the guilty.

What about Numbers 14:18: "The Lord is longsuffering, and of great mercy, forgiving iniquity and transgression, and by no means clearing the guilty, visiting the iniquity of the fathers upon the children unto the third and fourth generation." These children did not have "culpability" for those sins of the fathers. "Culpability" is a legal and theological term which means they did not bear responsibility because they were directly to blame for the evil; but, indirectly, they shared in the consequences of the evil.

Every son and daughter of Adam is still sharing in the basic curses of the fall: the curse on the ground (thorns and thistles); death (unto dust shall thou return); the woman shall bear the sorrow of childbirth; and the man shall earn his living by the "sweat of his brow" (Genesis 3:14-19). You can rest assured that as of this date, man, everyman, Christian and non-Christian still suffer from the curses enumerated here.

Weeds still grow in the Christian's lawn, just like they do the non-Christian's. I am not saying that God cannot and will not, on occasion, give a special blessing to His people; but ride past some hyper-spiritual saint's house and see if he does not have the same problem with his lawn that you have with yours. Childbearing is still accomplished by suffering.

And we could multiply the examples further. The child of God has a right to call upon God, and even to expect God to bless Him in his moments of need; but the fact remains that the child of God must face these difficulties just like everyone else.

Now the curse in Genesis chapter three that was pronounced upon man was not the absolute, perfect will of God for man. The perfect will of God was evidenced in the earlier chapters: there man did not have to worry about weeds; apparently if children were to come into the earth, God had a plan that was different from the normal means of childbirth as we know it; and even death was, apparently, not in God's arrangements for mankind. Here we have a picture of God's **perfect** will for man; and in chapter three we have a picture of God's **permissive** will for man.

But was the curse of Genesis three removed; or is the curse of the law removed? I know of some faith people who believe that they do not even have to worry about roaches getting into their houses. They do not believe they will get sick, and some believe they will live to at least 70 years of age, in perfect health; and to top that off some are now believing they will never die. How can they believe this? Because they say the "curse" has been removed, and they have claimed their deliverance from any effect of that curse - especially, the curse of the law.

I am not sure that I understand what they believe is encompassed under the word "curse." But, friend, if you are going to be spared an infestation of cockroaches, go ahead and believe that your wife will be spared the pangs of childbirth. I have not read of anyone claiming the latter.

Well, what about this matter of being delivered from the curse? Is a Christian delivered from the curse of the law, or every curse? The passage most often used to explain deliverance from the "curse of the law" is found in Galatians: "Christ hath redeemed us from the curse of the law, being made a curse for us" (Galatians 3:13). Well this verse certainly does say that "Christ hath redeemed us (Christians) from the 'curse of the law'."

Only two questions remain to be answered: what is the "curse," and in what sense have we been delivered from that curse? The "faith teachers" refer this verse back to Deuteronomy chapter 28, which delineates a number of curses, among these are quite a few sicknesses. Let us make a few comments.

I picked up a dozen commentaries, by good, evangelical scholars, and none of them referred Galatians chapter 3 back to Deuteronomy chapter 28. To do so is poor Biblical interpretation and an unbalanced approach to Scriptural exegesis. Galatians three makes it clear that the "curse of the law" they referred to is the condemnation for depending upon the law for salvation. That condemnation or curse is found in Romans 3:23, "For the wages of sin is death..." (Romans 3:23). "Death" means spiritual death, not physical death.

Galatians 3:10 is a quotation of Deuteronomy 27:26, but the reference is merely one of saying that trying to keep the law for salvation will bring a curse upon him or her who attempts to do so. In other words, Galatians chapter three is dealing with the subject of salvation, "The just shall live by faith" (Galatians 3:11).

Furthermore, Deuteronomy chapter 28 is a specific command to a specific people (Israel), that offers rewards for obedience, and curses for disobedience. It is improper to take isolated passages of Scripture and apply them randomly to any and everybody. One can prove that God wants to heal, in my opinion, by utilizing Scripture verses that are directly applicable, and not by resorting to proof texting.

It is true that Christ has redeemed us from the "curse" of any and every law; whatever that curse may be. But again, the full and final resolution of the effects of sin is future: particularly note the book of Revelation, Millennial passages, and other pertinent Scriptures.

We do not want to overemphasize one point, but I believe that God can, and does want to make provision for any and every need that a Christian has: within the framework of mortality and His present permissive will. The Christian may, and should pray, and under normal circumstances expect deliverance; this is Scriptural.

But the point that we must not forget is this: Man is a needy creature; God may deliver him today, and he will likely have another need for tomorrow. And no kind of theory or explanation of faith that makes faith a mere tool to manipulate God, and to turn the Almighty into a glorified bellhop, can be substantiated by the Bible. Every doctrinal explanation, without fail, must preserve the sovereignty of the Almighty.

Now, we must conclude that God has established laws, "codes and rules of conduct," by which even He must live. In order to be faithful to Himself, God must be consistent in His thinking and in His works and the execution of His laws.

Furthermore, enroute to His final and glorious purpose of ultimate and absolute redemption, God has found it necessary to permit man to live in the kind of world you and I live in – a not too beautiful world on occasion. And, even though God has made some very glorious provisions and has given some exceedingly great promises to His children, and has allowed them to "taste the good word of God, and the powers of the world to come" (Hebrews 6:5), it still rains on the just and the unjust, and Christians as well as non-Christians must, on occasion, suffer.

Therefore, the execution of the laws of God do permit suffering. But it is difficult to believe that God would permit anything to come up on a child of His that did not, or could not, have meaning for that child. It is not our purpose to get into the matter of suffering – that is, what benefits can accrue to the child of God from it; but let us briefly look at the subject.

First of all, I believe Paul E. Billheimer's book, *Don't Waste Your Sorrows*, does a stupendous job of opening up this important area. The title, in itself, should be quite meaningful. But suffering, and why should we exclude physical suffering, has a purpose.

The writer to the Hebrews, in chapter 12, constantly reminds us that we are in a period of child training, through the chastening of the heavenly Father. He did not indicate that it would be pleasurable; to the contrary – he said, "Now no chastening for the present to be joyous, but grievous" (Hebrews 12:11). And the apostle Paul said, "For our light affliction, which is but for a moment, worketh for us a far more exceeding and eternal weight of glory" (II Corinthians 4:17). And Paul stated on another occasion that his "thorn in the flesh" was sent to keep him humble (II Corinthians 12:7).

And we must not forget what the writer to the Hebrews said about Jesus Christ. Hebrews 5:8: "Though he were a Son, yet learned he obedience by the things which he suffered." Simon Peter said, "Wherefore let them that suffer according to the will of God," indicating that the suffering for righteousness' sake was something God was fully conscious of, and was in accord with.

Do these kinds of answers completely satisfy me? Absolutely Not. And perhaps this side of heaven you and I shall not receive the answer to some of our puzzling questions about suffering. Perhaps we shall not be able to understand the reasons for some of our suffering, in the same manner that God permitted Joseph to understand his. Joseph, after all his trials and tribulations, was permitted to say, "But as for you, ye thought evil against me, but God meant it unto good, to bring to pass, as it is this day, to save much people alive" (Genesis 50:20). But the song says, "We'll understand it better, bye and bye."

...we can never compartmentalize God's thoughts, and plans, and will in neat little theological packages...

10

Why People Are Not Healed

What are some of the reasons people are not healed? The Bible certainly lays down a number of these; but it is also our opinion that it is totally impossible to fathom the depths of the infinite mind of the Almighty God, and, hence, to completely understand why He acts as He always does. Isaiah 55:8 says, "For my thoughts are not your thoughts, neither are your ways my ways, saith the Lord."

Can we not learn that we can never compartmentalize God's thoughts, and plans, and will in neat little theological packages; and that to even attempt to distill the mind of God and summarize it in little books, with the understanding that we have completely fathomed that mind, is nothing more than an affront to the Almighty God.

But we are permitted to "study the Word of God" and to "teach and preach" those things that are contained therein. That, obviously, will permit a limited understanding of the divine truth. Here, then, are what we believe to be some Biblical statements as to why healing does not take place.

(1) Men are oftentimes not healed because of sin.
Psalm 66:18 says, "If I regard iniquity in my heart, the Lord will not hear me." The word "regard" has several meanings:

such as "to see," and even "to enjoy when one sees something." To say that God, absolutely, never hears the prayer of a sinner or a person with sin in his life, does not always hold true. But I believe that the Psalmist, who, by the way, oftentimes sinned, is saying that one who knowingly, willingly, is harboring sin in his or her life (or any fault or failure), is not a real candidate for an answer to prayer. Suffice to say that under normal circumstances anyone who desires heavenly blessings would certainly want to confess known and unknown sin before approaching God for a blessing.

(2) **Failure to pray.** Prayer is the divinely appointed way to approach God. Mark 11:24 says, "What things so ever ye desire, when ye pray..." We covered the matter of prayer in detail in an earlier study, but prayer is the key that unlocks the door to God's storehouse of good treasures. Prayer prepares the heart and life of man, and permits God to release the power and blessings of heaven upon our lives and into our circumstances.

It is also the means of bringing about victory in the realm of the enemy, the unseen forces, the "principalities and powers" against whom we fight. Prayer is an indispensible weapon in our arsenal of fighting equipment. Certainly God could do anything with our without man and his prayers; but God, certainly on most occasions, simply has not chosen to act unless prayer has been unleashed toward heaven.

(3) **Failure to ask.** God also operates on the principle that men must ask for His assistance. Since God created man to be a free-willed creature, God will not intrude in man's affairs unless man seeks His assistance.

I John 5:14 says, "And this is the confidence that we have in him, that, if we ask…" Matthew 7:7 says, "Ask, and it shall be given you; seek, and ye shall find; knock, and it shall be opened unto you: For every one that asketh receiveth; and he that seeketh findeth; and to him that knocketh it shall be opened" (Matthew 7:7-8). Ask, seek, knock – all these indicate a persistent, constant, pleading for the blessings of God.

(4) **Praying in the will of God.** I John 5:14-15: "And this is the confidence that we have in him, that, if we ask anything according to his will, he heareth us: and if we know that he hear us, whatsoever we ask, we know that we have the petitions that we desired of him." This matter of praying in the will of God has been covered under the subject of the "will of God." But suffice it to say, a prayer prayed outside the will of God does not have the promise that it shall be answered.

Again, we are not going to be dogmatic and say God never does give things that are not according to His will; certainly He has and does grant things that are not according to His perfect or absolute will. An indication of this is to be found in Psalm 106:13-15 which says, "They soon forgot his works; they waited not for his counsel: But lusted exceedingly in the wilderness, and tempted God in the desert. And he gave them their request; but sent leanness into their soul."

The fact is based on good Biblical basis that states that God sometimes gives or permits or allows the second best because of the obstinacy of men's hearts. You remember that God granted Israel's request for a king; when, in reality this was not His perfect will for them. But if a person can pray in the perfect will of God, we can believe that God does hear that individual. And the certainty of an answer is guaranteed. But let us offer this caution: there is always a Scripture verse somewhere that will demolish our neat little theological packages and pat formulas.

(5) **Failure to abide in Him.** John 15:7 says, "If ye abide in me, and my word abide in you, ye shall ask what ye will, and it shall be dune unto you." We have, in this verse, the secret to why much prayer is unanswered. This verse also should help to clear up a seeming contradiction between what many of us believe, and what the Bible, on the other hand, seems to teach.

I have read many Scripture verses which seem to be absolute, unequivocal statements that God would do certain things if I just believed, just had faith. I then proceeded to believe and mustered all the human faith I could arouse: but nothing happened. I often wondered, "Why?" Why the unanswered prayer?

The answer is, first of all, that we must balance the Word; me must take into account all the Scriptures that speak about or deal with the matters of faith and prayer and the reception of divine blessings. Here is a key element that must be taken into consideration. There is a Biblical principle of "abiding." And to "abide" is to remain in; it, essentially, means to be one with, to agree with.

We mentioned this point previously, but it bears repeating. I often wondered why Jesus Christ always had His prayer requests answered; but, on the other hand, it is doubtful any man ever had all his requests answered. The answer is to be found at this point: the Bible says that Jesus and the Father were one. They were in such oneness of relationship that the mind of Christ and the mind of the Father were always thinking the same thing.

Therefore when Christ asked the Father for something, He was always praying and asking in the perfect will of God. And you and I are, at best, weak, frail human beings. And no matter what our motivation is, much of the time we stay in bondage to the flesh (the body), and our minds and hearts are clouded to the eternal purposes and will of Almighty God. But when we are in a position of "abiding"; that is, our mind and heart and will are flowing in unanimity of purpose with God, then and then only, we can ask what we will and it will (without exception or doubt) be done. Paise The Lord!

Now, are you not seeing some of the simplistic interpretations that much of the faith school is doing being exploded at this point? Do you not see that if, as a human being, you could perfectly abide or remain in that oneness relationship with God, then you could always have every prayer answered.

But, conversely, the reason every prayer would be answered, would be conditioned on the fact that you knew perfectly the will of God, and always prayed according to that will. In my opinion some saints do reach a high level of "abiding relationship; and, consequently, they do have a great number of prayers answered.

For instance, there is a precious verse out of the Old Testament that is applicable at this point. Psalm 37:4 says, "Delight thyself also in the Lord; and he shall give thee the desires of thy heart." What the Psalmist is saying is: that if you delight yourself in God and His will and His plans for you, and if you so surrender yourself to His plan for your life, so that you and the Lord see "eye-to-eye" (as one man said); God can then afford to give you anything you ask from Him. But, of course, you will be asking only those things that are in conformity to His will.

It is foolish to choose verses like Psalm 37:4 and make them indicate that God will grant any frivolous, foolish thing that pops in one's mind. No, God could not grant such things. But He does promise to grant our desires: those desires that proceed from a heart that is in unity and oneness with God's will and purpose.

(6) **Failure to pray in Jesus' Name.** Now many of the reasons are tied together, but there is yet a significant difference in them. Often, for instance, we are told to pray in Jesus' Name. John 14:13, 14 says, "And whatsoever ye shall ask in my name, that will I do, that the Father may be glorified in the Son. If ye shall ask any thing in my name, I will do it." And John 16:24, "Hitherto have ye asked nothing in my name: ask and ye shall receive, that your joy may be full."

These verses tell us that if we ask something in the name of Jesus, God will grant it. Have you not often prayed, then closed your prayer with the pat little formula, "In Jesus' name," and then received nothing? But asking in Jesus' name is not merely the use of a formula to evoke a magic solution. More is involved.

To pray in Jesus' name is to use that name in the same sense that Jesus would use it; it is to append His name to only that with which He Himself would give approval. In this sense, then, it is to pray for that which is in the will of God. It may be true that we have been granted a "power of attorney," but a "power of attorney" has restrictions and limitations placed upon it. It should never exceed the wishes and will of the grantor.

We could never expect Jesus' to endorse just anything and everything that men pray for. If we truly pray and put Jesus' name on something it should be something He can endorse; something that is in conformity to His will; hence, something with which the "Father may be glorified in the Son."

Notice, there are no limitations to what we can ask for: "If ye shall ask any thing in my name..." The secret to "answered prayer" is being in such tune with the mind and will and purpose of Almighty God that one can ask in conformity with His will.

(7) **Lack of faith.** Most of the time our failure to receive from God probably lies at this point – lack of faith. Mark 11:22 says, "Have faith in God." Hebrews 11:6, "Without faith it is impossible to please him..." Matthew 17:20 says, "If ye have faith as a grain of a mustard seed, ye shall say unto this mountain, Remove hence to yonder place; and it shall remove; and nothing shall be impossible unto you."

Faith, simply stated, is trust and belief; there are other elements, but this is essentially the meaning of the Word. Since we have discussed faith elsewhere, we shall limit our remarks. But let us mention several brief, but important points.

First, let our faith be properly placed. "Faith in faith" will disappoint you; while "faith in God" will never disappoint. Faith in God simply means that we pray to, and trust in, an infinite, all knowing, wise Being for our needs. If, for some reason, our requests are not granted in the manner we ask; we recognize that there are other purposes and involvements that God has taken into consideration – therefore we must trust **our** God: not **our** faith. Many folk would be saved disappointments at this point if they were to understand this truth.

Second, our human faith can grow and mature. We can be faith people and have a mixture of faith and unbelief.

This was true of the disciples in Matthew 17:14-20. The disciples had enough human faith to attempt to bring about a cure of a lunatic man; but still Jesus had to chide them for their "unbelief" (verse 20). The Bible speaks of "great faith" (Matthew 8:10), and of "little faith" (Matthew 8:26), and a need to "increase our faith" (Luke 17:5). Thus there are levels and degrees of faith.

I have often said that I believe people who never have doubts, or, at least, say they never do, have died and gone to heaven and do not know it yet. Our prayer has to continually be, "Lord, help thou my unbelief." In other words, increase my faith.

Thirdly, faith operates in an environment. This is a truth I discovered some time ago that has been quite meaningful to me. Webster's defines the word "environment" as "something that surrounds," and "all the conditions, circumstances, and influences surrounding, and affecting the development of" something. Our simplistic faith friends, with their unbalanced approach to scripture, fail to take this into consideration.

Faith is affected by many things: the spiritual condition of my heart, my prayer life, the amount of, and maturity of development of my faith, and a number of other elements. To merely say, "Have faith, confess it, it is done," fails to take into consideration of all these important elements of faith.

If one has a difficult time believing this, just let that one read I Corinthians 13 for an example. Paul said, "...and though I have all faith, so that I could remove mountains, and have not charity, I am nothing..." (verse 2). The genuineness of my faith is conditioned by many other things. And there is one Biblical principle that needs expression in these days: One must take the "whole counsel of God."

And the concluding point we would make about faith is this: the healing of a person is not necessarily dependent upon that person's faith. Those people who pray for others and cast all blame on them for not being healed, are outside the Word of God in their assertions. As we have pointed out in James the 5th chapter, it is the prayer and faith of the elders that bring recovery.

If a lack of faith is sin, as some are saying, then the biggest sinners are those self-styled healers who hold mass healing crusades and send home people by the thousands who were not healed by their laying on of hands and their prayers. These men are simply pouring guilt upon the heads of innocent people who exercised all the faith they had; where was the faith of the one doing the praying? The use of Romans 14:23 to undergird this kind of teaching, is a totally false application of this verse and its context to the truth of healing.

As a matter of fact, it would appear that God sometimes heals without the faith of either the one praying or the one who is healed. We must recognize that God is a sovereign God; He does not always operate according to the standards of men. As a matter of fact, some of the great, documented healings that took place in Kathryn Kuhlman's crusades, were the healings of people, oftentimes, who went merely out of curiosity and who were healed when they were not even seeking healing. And it is doubtful that they were believers. Why good saints are bypassed is a puzzling question that only God knows the answer to.

But we still recognize that if we could develop our faith, our belief and trust in God, there is virtually no limit to what God could and would do in answer to our prayers.

(8) **A refusal to see medicine as a way that God heals.**
Now some of my faith friends would quickly discount this
point; as would some of my friends who have believed in
healing and the refusal of "means" (medicine) prior to the
newer, more modern interpretation of the healing process.
I praise God for people who trust in God; if this means
trusting God without the use of medicine and doctors, God
bless them. But, personally, this is not my understanding of
Scripture.

First, I do not believe that one can separate God's
creation into the secular and the sacred (this is the biggest
mistake the church is making today – everything is sacred if
it is dedicated to God).

Secondly, as someone else has said, "Nature is
God's ordinary way of doing a thing, and a miracle is His
extraordinary way of doing it. It is as much the work of God
to produce grapes filled with juice as it is to turn water into
wine. Only God could do either. Paul may plant and Apollos
may water, but only God can give the increase." And, "God
seems to invoke miracle only, or chiefly, when natural means
are inadequate." I believe that a miracle is the imposition of
a higher law; not the rejection of law.

Thirdly, James 1:17 says, "Every good gift and every
perfect gift is from above, and cometh down from the Father
of lights, with whom is no variableness, neither shadow of
turning." Simply stated: nothing is in and of itself evil; the
use determines the good or bad of an object.

Paul wrote to Timothy and said there are those who
are "commanding to abstain from meats, which God hath
created to be received with thanksgiving of them which
believe and know the truth. For every creature of God
is good, and nothing to be refused, if it be received with

thanksgiving" (I Timothy 4:3-5). The NIV properly renders
verse 4, "For **everything** God created is good, and nothing
is to be rejected if it is received with thanksgiving." And,
Genesis 1:31 says, "And God saw everything that he had
made, and, behold, it was very good..."

Fourthly, the Bible makes it plain that God heals
in answer to prayer; He heals where there is no prayer
by the recuperative powers of nature; and He heals,
as in Hezekiah's case, by the use of means (medicinal
substances).

Now the first objection to the use of medicine and
doctors is that this is a lack of faith. I use to buy that; but I
do not feel that it rings true. It appears to me that this kind
of thinking could result from a superficial understanding
of faith. As someone said, "Beauty is in the eye of the
beholder." Who can really say that God gets more glory out
of a direct healing without medicine than He does out of
healing with medicine?

Any good doctor worth his salt will tell you he cannot
heal anyone; he can supply his knowledge and skill, but,
even an unbelieving physician will say that nature must do
the healing (we understand of course that God is behind
nature; therefore, why is not God the healer?). So to say
that one gives more glory to God than does the other, is
simply the way one looks at it. In both cases, with or without
medicine, God is the healer!

Now in the case of Asa (II Chronicles 16:12, 13),
the Bible says that "he sought not to the Lord, but to the
physicians." And as a result he died. But this must not
be taken as an absolute command of God in light of other
Scriptures. As a matter of fact, it appears that the problem
was that he simply bypassed God altogether. Certainly

Christians should consult God before they consult anybody else about their problems and needs.

An interesting statement is found in the book of Ecclesiastes (one of the apocryphal books) which says that after we pray we should let the doctor take over and "do not let him leave you, for you need him. Sometimes success is in their hands, since they in turn will beseech the Lord to grant them the grace to relieve and to heal, that life may be saved" (Ecclesiastes 38:12-14).

Is it really a lack of faith to consult a physician? Yes, if you have not gone to God first with your need. No, if this seems to be the way that God leads in your situation. What does it mean not to have faith, anyway? I heard of a preacher, whom I know, who was giving up a situation where he had a good salary and a good housing allowance. He said, "I am now going to live by faith; I am entering into a 'faith-walk'."

Well, that sounded good to me, until I saw through the flimsiness of such statements. Men say, over the radio and television, we have a "faith ministry"; please send your support, Now, the question is, "what kind of definition of faith are they talking about?"

Well, negatively, they are saying that a non-ministerial person, who works for a living, is not living by faith (let us be logical). Or, a minister who draws a regular salary is not "walking by faith," while an evangelist or radio minister, or the like, is living or walking by faith. Nonsense! It takes faith to believe God will provide through the means of a regular salary, just like it does if the income is not a weekly paycheck. Faith is faith is faith. The truth is they are giving the word "faith" a special, non-Biblical definition.

These folks are saying that their faith is in God to work through people; while those with weekly salaries have their faith in men to provide (pray tell me what the difference is?). This is a poor understanding of faith. Most Christians I know who work on jobs have just as much faith that God provides, even though it comes through an employer, as do the people who must appeal to committed Christians to supply their needs. This "faith walk" thing is too often a smoke screen that attempts to cast an aura of "I'm somebody special; I'm a faith person; I live by a faith-walk."

Every genuine, committed child of God ought to be a faith person in a faith-walk. I am no more of a faith person now than I was when I draw a regular salary from a pastorate; even thought my needs sometimes seem to be greater and my supply less. But I am a faith person, not on the basis of where my income comes from; but I am a faith-person on the basis of how much faith I have in God!

The same point applies to the use of doctors and medicine. If your faith is in the doctor and the medicine, then God can receive little direct glory. But if your faith is in God to utilize the services of the physician and his medicine, then "to God be the glory, great things He hath done." We, too often, have built doctrines on questionable Scriptural evidence.

Read Isaiah chapter 38. King Hezekiah, a man who said, "I have walked before thee in truth and with a perfect heart, and have done that which is good in thy sight..." prayed when he was "sick unto death." The Bible says that God said, "I have heard thy prayer... I will add unto thy days fifteen years." Now, how did God do this? Isaiah 38:21 says, "For Isaiah had said, Let them take a lump of figs, and lay it for a plaster upon the boil, and he shall recover."

God used means (medicine). And this was administered in response to a *"rhema"* (direct word) to his prophet, Isaiah.

Further, II Kings 20 tells us that by the third day King Hezekiah was well enough to go to the house of the Lord. It was not even instant healing; but God did use means to bring about healing; and it was "divine healing."

In I Timothy 5:23 the Holy Spirit spoke through Paul and told him to tell Timothy to "Drink no longer water, but use a little wine for thy stomach's sake and thine often infirmities." The debate over whether this was wine with alcohol, or grape juice, is insignificant for our purposes. The wine was to be used as a medicine. If juice can be pressed from grapes and used for healing; why cannot the syrup be pressed out of the castor bean and used for a medicine?

You see, sometimes Jesus spoke a word and men were healed, other times He, Jesus, used means. He used a spittle mixed with clay to heal a blind man. He used a fish, and a hook, and Peter, to get money for taxes (Matthew 17:27). He used five loaves and two small fishes to feed the five thousand. He used a donkey to ride into Jerusalem when He could have used a heavenly chariot. Why should Jesus not use means, medicine, for the divine healing of His saints in answer to prayer when He so chooses.

The newspapers constantly carry articles about ministers who insist that their people cease taking medicine and stop seeing physicians, and who subsequently die. These kind of rash statements and opinions only bring reproach to the kingdom of God. It is simply unscriptural to knowingly set up opposition between doctors and medicine and God. Thank God for the good medical doctors and chiropractic physicians who first lay their hands on their patients in believing prayer before they utilize their God-given skills.

(9) **Men ask amiss.** James 4:3 says, "Ye ask, and receive not, because ye ask amiss that ye may consume it upon your own lusts." The word amiss means wrongly, even wickedly. This verse speaks of a selfish motive in asking something from God. Too many people seek healing, or other blessing, with the wrong motive in mind. They make a world of promises to God; and then, when God heals, they dissipate their energies and squander their God-given strength on unrighteous causes. But, and I cannot understand it, God will sometimes grant healing to those kind of people.

(10) **Because of doubt about the will of God.** This point is somewhat similar to the point we discussed about praying in the will of God; however, there is some difference. If a person does not believe that God really wants to heal him, then there is going to be no solid basis for trust and belief. We have dealt lengthily with the Scriptural basis for healing, and the will of God in this matter; however, a couple of statements are in order.

First, if there were no Scriptures explicitly offering healing, the general promises in the Bible to God's people should be sufficient evidence that God wants to bless His people in the matter of divine healing.

Second, James 1:6, 7 says, "But let him ask in faith, nothing wavering. For he that wavereth is like a wave of the sea driven with the wind and tossed. For let not that man think that he shall receive any thing of the Lord." No Scripture that I am aware of ever tells us **not** to pray for healing; there are always positive admonitions to seek for healing blessings.

And, it is generally agreed, by good Scriptural scholars, that it is best not to place at the end of one's request, "If it be thy will." While, properly understood, I find no fault with this; it would, perhaps, be better to append, as Agnes Sanford suggests, "Let this be done according to Your will."

While there may only be a slight difference in the two statements; the second statement does recognize that the one praying does not understand or know all the factors involved, and that God may delay, or refuse, the healing on the basis of some things that we are not aware of. But we must believe that God's perfect will is for healing; and that we have a right and duty to ask for that healing.

(11) **A refusal to depend upon the Holy Spirit for assistance.** Oh, how we need to look to the assistance of the Comforter. Romans 8:26, 27 says, "Likewise the Spirit also helpeth our infirmities: for we know not what we should pray for as we ought: but the Spirit itself maketh intercession which cannot be uttered. And he that searcheth the hearts knoweth what is the mind of the Spirit, because he maketh intercession for the saints according to the will of God." The Holy Spirit can always pray according to the will of God; whereas we cannot. But the main fact is we need the Comforter, the "parakletos" (meaning the "one called alongside"), to assist us in the vital needs that we approach God with.

(12) **A neglect to seek the assistance of others.** Matthew 18:19 says, "Again I say unto you, That if two of you shall agree on earth as touching any thing that they shall ask, it shall be done for them of my Father which is in heaven." Now this is not an absolute command that must always be observed; but it is an additional encouragement to the child of God. In agreement with what was said earlier,

if there is a direct leading of the Lord that something is the will of God, it would become an additional source of encouragement when two people feel the same burden and are in agreement that they are praying in the will of God. One person might check the other in order to determine that the prayer is not selfish. James says, "Confess your faults one to another, and pray one for another, that ye may be healed."

(13) **Failure to persist.** Luke 18:7, 8 says, "And shall not God avenge his own elect, which cry day and night unto him, though he bear long with them? I tell you that he will avenge them speedily…" For our "confess it, have faith, ye are healed" friends, they can find no comfort in this Scripture for their pray one time theory that says that any praying beyond that constitutes doubt. As matter of fact, in Luke 18 we read these words, "…men ought always to pray, and not to faint…" In most cases persistence in prayer is needed to bring results.

(14) **Failure to fast.** Matthew 17:21, in referring to the failure of the disciples to cure a young man, Jesus said, "Howbeit this kind goeth not out but by prayer and fasting." Fasting is one of the most neglected means of getting through to God; the lack of fasting is a sure indication that men and women are not totally sold-out to God's cause. Hence, much of our failure must lie at this point.

(15) **Failure to remove hindrances.** Matthew 5:23, 24 says, "If thou bring thy gift to the altar, and there rememberest that thy brother hath ought against thee; leave there thy gift before the altar, and go thy way; first be reconciled to thy brother, and then come and offer thy gift." Broken relationships need to be restored; obligations

satisfied and wrongs righted; hindrances removed – before we come to the altar with our gifts and our prayer requests.

(16) **Failure to observe the natural laws of God.** Proverbs 17:22, "A merry heart doeth good like a medicine: but a broken spirit drieth the bones." The Bible has many principles that speak to our daily health needs. The above verse is consistent with what we know about a positive attitude and the effects of such an attitude on the well being of the mind.

Dietary laws, though not applicable in this dispensation, still have vital truths in them. Overeating is forbidden, and, in general, we are cautioned to be moderate in all things. There is a good, renewed emphasis by many Christians on health foods, exercise, and other beneficial things that can bring glory to God through our bodies. "Know ye not that ye are the temple of the Holy Ghost..." Enough said.

These are just a number of the many reasons why people are not healed. But we still must remember that our faith must be "in God"; that is, in His wisdom and sovereign will and purposes, and that the God of all men will do what is right.

11

Faith: A Definition

What is the meaning of the word "faith?" I heard a preacher say that, "faith was not looking at the mountain, it was listening for the splash!" Norman Grubb said, "Faith is not the banishing of all difficulties, but their subordination to greater certainties."

But the word "faith," as we find it in the New Testament is translated from several related Greek words. **Pistis** is used 243 times in the New Testament and is always rendered "faith" with only 4 exceptions. The Greek word **pisteou** occurs 246 times and is almost always translated "believe." These two words are derived from **peitho,** meaning to persuade, to cause belief in a thing. It is used 55 times in the New Testament.

Vine says that the word "faith" means, "...primarily, a firm persuasion, a conviction based upon hearing, as used in the New Testament, always of faith in God or Christ, or things spiritual."

Therefore, to have faith is to have a firm conviction, to believe, to trust. Faith, for instance, is believing, and believing is to have faith. Faith is to be persuaded, to have belief in something. Faith is an act of the heart, so it includes the intellectual, the emotional, and the volitional or the willing faculties of man. The meaning of the word "faith," by definition, is not difficult to understand.

The closest the Bible comes to a definition of faith is in Hebrews 11:1 which says, "Now faith is in the substance of things hoped for, the evidence of things not seen." The writer in Hebrews is saying that "faith" or belief or firm assurance is "what is set or stands under" (or gives a foundation to) that which is only hoped for, which has not yet actually arrived.

The same word for substance **(hupostasis)** is used in Hebrews 1:3 which says, that Christ was "the express (very) image of" God's person or substance **(hupostasis).** When you have seen Christ you have seen the Father; Christ is the visible expression of His heavenly Father. Faith, then, is the "underlying reality," the foundation of what we hope for. Therefore faith is real; faith is a substance.

This faith, according to Hebrews 11:1 is the evidence, proof, conviction of those things which are not seen. Therefore "faith" relates us to the invisible. Hebrews 11:3 tells us how: "Through faith we understand that the worlds were framed by the word of God, so that things which are seen were not made of things which do appear."

Now these bodily senses relate us to the visible world. We can see it, feel it, hear it, taste it, and so forth. But, according to the Bible, the world we see (the visible world), was not made out of visible things. Faith draws back the curtain; it shows us what is behind all those things out there – the visible things.

There is a "human" faith, of course. And we use it; and rightly so. I am now looking at my watch; I have every reason to believe it is approximately correct. I hear my typewriter buzzing, so I have every reasonable belief, by my human faith, to believe the typewriter is working. That is human faith (faith without spiritual connotations). But, in the Bible, faith is related to two things, things not visible to the human eye: they are – God and His Word.

Faith does not, cannot, exist on the basis of what is seen. II Corinthians 5:7 says, "For we walk by faith, not by sight." Faith is the antithesis, the opposite, of sight. The world says that "seeing is believing." Missouri is the show-me state; but the Christian faith-walk reverses it and says, "believing is seeing."

Psalm 27:13 as given by David says, "I had fainted, unless I had believed to see the goodness of the Lord in the land of the living." David believed, then he saw the goodness of the Lord. Follow that roll call of the saints in Hebrews 11. It says, "By faith the walls of Jericho fell down, after...they were compassed about seven days." And on and on and on. Faith, belief, then the appearance of the invisible.

Faith gives substance to that which is not seen, and makes it real. But "faith" in God's Word and in God, gives a foundation to those things which we are hoping and praying for, the things of the unseen realm. Just as words are an expression of a person; thus the Bible is an expression of God. These are the source of our faith and belief. An important note: the **Word is not God** – it is an expression of God. There is some confusion that is being spread at this point by some teachers; we shall say more about this later.

II Corinthians 4:17, 18 gives us further examples of this visible and invisible problem: "For by our light affliction, which is but for a moment, worketh for us a far more exceeding and eternal weight of glory: While we look not at the things which are not seen: for the things which are seen are temporal; but the things which are not seen are eternal."

We can only "look" at the things which are not seen by faith; and we can only do this "while" we are not looking at the visible, the circumstantial world. We will have afflictions; I see no reason to believe this might not include some sickness and infirmities. And if then these come we continue to look to the unseen realm by faith, these afflictions will secure us "an eternal weight of glory."

Now that we have looked at the meaning of the word "faith," let us recognize quite an important fact: **there are several different kinds of faith or expressions of faith.** Let us look at them:

1. There is a NATURAL faith or belief that every man has. As we pointed out earlier, and as Norman Grubb says, "The difference is in the object of the faith." That is probably an over-simplification, nonetheless, it does tell us a lot about the meaning of "faith." All men have the ability to believe; we could not live without that ability. And by this we mean the ability to believe without total evidence in the object. Men, for instance, ride elevators, airplanes, and the like – in so doing they exercise a degree of faith.

There is even a natural faith that believes in God (but this in only an intellectual, head faith). James 2:19 says, "Thou believest that there is one God; thou doest well: the devils also believe and tremble." Someone has said that the demons are probably more orthodox in their beliefs than some professing Christians. Even Simon Magus, in Acts the 8th chapter, "believed also" (Acts 8:13), nevertheless, "...thy heart is not right" (Acts 8:21).

2. There is a SAVING FAITH. These kinds of faith are not, actually, different faiths; but they are special degrees or applications of faith that produce different things or have special uses. The Bible separates the uses of faith; so the question is, "Why should we not separate them?" John 3:16 says, "For God so loved the world, that he gave his only begotten Son, that whosoever believeth in him should not perish, but have eternal life." This is the faith that is considered the condition and instrument of salvation.

Let us pose this question: "Is not faith the gift of God?" Dr. Adam Clark answers this to my satisfaction. "Yes, (faith is the gift of God), as to the grace by which it is produced; but the grace or power to believe, and the act of believing are two different things. Without the grace or power to believe no man ever did or can believe; but with that power the act of faith is a man's own. God never believes, for any man, no more than He repents for him."

A beautiful thing about the free will of man is this: God will not manipulate man (hence, man must receive the gift of grace); any more than man can manipulate God (hence faith can be said to be a gift of God). As a matter of fact, the power to believe must be present long before man actually does believe; else why the constant threats from Scripture to condemn and judge man, if, in fact, that man is not able to believe.

Now the question my faith teaching friends must answer is this, "If, without exception, a man or woman repents, confesses his sins and believes and is immediately and without exception saved (and I have never read or heard anyone dispute this: although, all things being equal, there is probably someone somewhere who would do so); then why cannot we say with equal assurance, "Repent, believe and be healed?" And the healing would be received as instantaneously as the salvation.

The burden of the responsibility for this answer is on their backs. Let us state, in general terms, what we believe is the truth about this matter: healing is not in the atonement in the sense that salvation from sins is; and simple faith is not the only reason people are not healed. There are obviously other reasons for not getting healed, other than those proposed by the "have faith, confess it, ye are healed" folk who say, "You just did not have faith."

3. The PRAYER OF FAITH. We discussed this kind of faith in an earlier session, but let us review it. James 5:14, 15 says, "Is any sick among you? Let him call for the elders of the church; and let them pray over him, anointing him with oil in the name of the Lord: And the prayer of faith shall save the sick, and the Lord shall raise him up; and if he have committed sins, they shall be forgiven him."

A brief summary of our previous statement is this: the "prayer of faith" is a supernatural gift of faith to a group of elders (I would not limit it to such a situation entirely, God will always tear up our formulas), who are praying for the ill. Following the formula in James 5 (of course there could be reasons for not being able to absolutely follow the prescribed pattern; i.e. oil may not be readily available etc.); but seeking to follow this pattern as closely as possible, this group seeks for divine intervention to bring about a "divine healing."

The statements are very positive in this passage; and if the "prayer of faith is prayed," the Lord shall raise the individual up, and he shall be healed. One small point of interest which I believe we failed to mention earlier in our consideration of this passage: Verse 13 says, "Is any among you afflicted? Let him pray..." In other words, for minor things, this passage suggests that the one afflicted may do his or her praying without calling on anyone else.

4. The GIFT OF FAITH. We find an example of this in I Corinthians 12:9: "To another faith by the same spirit…" Now I believe there is a basic difference between the "gift of faith," and the "prayer of faith." Many Bible students do not recognize this. They advance their conclusions on the assumption that all faith is a gift of God; hence, one faith cannot be distinguished from another faith.

It is true that the supernatural element of faith that flows from God's grace must always come from God, or else all the belief in the world on the part of man will produce nothing. But there is an essential difference between the "prayer of faith" and the "gift of faith." The "prayer of faith" is arrived at, usually, in a group situation, following the procedures outlined in James, chapter 5. While the "gift of faith" is one of the 9 gifts of the Spirit, the charismata of I Corinthians chapter 12. One is exercised in a group setting; the other is exercised by an individual.

Thus the "gift of faith" is given by God to a person, whom we like to refer to as having a "ministry in a specific gift." It is not a permanent possession; it is not an individual's to command; it may only be properly manifested as "the Spirit wills." It is, in my opinion, designated to be used within the body of believers. Again we want to refrain from dogmatism.

This gift of faith, in the setting outlined in I Corinthians 12, is dispensed by God for reasons that He alone, in His sovereign judgment, knows. To those who believe they can audaciously exercise faith to accomplish whatever they desire or want; let them turn to Jesus Christ for an example. John 5:19 says, "The Son can do nothing of himself, but what he seeth the Father do..." And again in John 14:10, "Believest thou not that I am in the Father, and the Father in me? The words that I speak unto you I speak not of myself: but the Father that dwelleth in me, he doeth the works."

How in the universe can we believe that we can indiscriminately do whatever meets or suits our fancy? We shall talk about the *"rhema"* and the *"logos,"* but there are other factors that we should take into consideration. Just as God will determine when and by whom and how the "gift of faith" is manifested; the same God will determine when and how and by whom **any** faith is manifested. As we pointed out, did not even the Son of God, Jesus Christ, the second person of the divine Godhead, subject Himself to the same considerations?

And notice, Jesus did not curse every fruitless fig tree (He only cursed one and that was for a lesson); He did not raise all the dead (think of the times He walked by graveyards and passed funeral processions, but declared, at least through His actions, that that was not the highest purpose to be served in behalf of humanity). And, by the way, Jesus did not heal everyone that He came in contact with. Matthew 14:58, in referring to a trip into His own country, says, "And he did not many mighty works there because of their unbelief."

But one problem has always puzzled me. In a sense Jesus did promise that we could do the works that He did. I always wondered why virtually everyone that Jesus prayed for was healed, while this is not true of any believer, no matter how gifted in a faith ministry he or she is. I saw at least part of that answer when I read John 10:30: Jesus said, "I and my Father are one." If we had that kind of relationship with Almighty God, there is no question we would know when and how to pray, and we would, consequently, see a greater manifestation of God's power.

5. FAITH AS A FRUIT. In Galatians 5:22, 23 we read: "But the fruit of the Spirit is love, joy, peace, longsuffering, gentleness, goodness, faith, meekness, temperance..." The basic difference between faith as a gift and faith as a fruit is this: faith as a gift expresses "ability"; while faith as a fruit expresses "character."

A good illustration, not original with me, is to picture a Christmas tree and an orange tree side by side. From a Christmas tree you will select gifts. That gift may be a book, a toy or whatever; that gift says nothing whatsoever about that Christmas tree. But from an orange tree you will pull an orange. That orange will tell you a great deal about the character of that tree. It will indicate how healthy that tree is, what variety of tree it is and so on. Jesus spoke of this in Matthew 7: "Even so every good tree bringeth forth good fruit; but a corrupt tree bringeth forth evil fruit. A good tree cannot bring forth evil fruit. Wherefore by their fruits ye shall know them" (Matthew 7:17, 18, 20).

Gifts as a fruit show what kind of trust and commitment we exhibit day in and day out in our Christian walk. The exercise of the gift of faith is a momentary act, and says little or nothing about the individual exercising it.

Why, then, the inordinate emphasis and exultation of people who exercise the more flashy gifts, when faith as a fruit is a true indication of spirituality? Those in the holiness tradition do not want to admit it, but God has, in times past, entrusted some questionable characters with gifts – both in and out of the Bible. But do we recognize that the exercise of a gift does not, in any way, indicate the character of an individual.

6. MINISTRY FAITH. Romans 12:3 reads, "For I say, through the grace given unto me, to every man that is among you, not to think of himself more highly than he ought to think; but to think soberly, according as God hath dealt to every man the measure of faith." Recognizing that God has dealt faith to us out of a bountiful supply of grace, we should not "think of (ourselves) more highly than (we ought)" (verse 3).

Every Christian has a measure of faith in order to perform some task in the body. It is for sure that if we find our place in the body, God has given us faith to carry out our appointed task. The important thing to recognize is this: every Christian has been given faith.

To say, "Well, I just do not have faith" is to contradict Scripture. You do have faith; you may or may not be using that faith, but it is resident in you, ready to be exercised in the channel God has outlined for your life. It is theologically and doctrinally unsound to say that a Christian "just did not have faith." Obviously, from what has already been said, and Biblically documented, the teaching that inspires this kind of thinking is unbalanced and unsound.

7. FAITH IN GOD, and **8. THE FAITH OF GOD.** We actually have two different applications of faith. There appears to be only a subtle difference, but there is a difference.

Some folk, for instance, say they believe; as a matter of fact that they indicate they have a great degree of faith in God's ability to do certain things. And, they are undoubtedly correct. But as we are seeing in our discussion of the various applications of faith, there are different ways in which faith can be given and applied.

As someone has said, faith is faith is faith: that is
Scripturally correct. But so is it true to say that electricity
is electricity is electricity. But there are different wattages,
different uses, different applications (to cook and to heat),
and so on.

Thus it is with faith. The Bible makes many distinctions
about the usages, applications, amounts and the like
of faith. Many people do have great "faith in God." But
ordinarily that kind of faith will not bring the healing miracle.

I can speak from experience on this score. I remember
praying for a blind boy. I believed with every ounce of
my human faith and belief; I believed that God was more
than abundantly able to bring about a restorative, creative
miracle – but nothing happened. That was "faith in God."
We need this kind of faith; we should attempt to exercise it
in the absence of one of the other forms of faith. And, after
all, every Christian worth his or her salt, believes that "God
can."

But let us notice a subtle, but most vital shift of words
in this next form of faith. In Mark 11:22-24 we read, "And
Jesus answering saith unto them, have faith in God. For
verily I say unto you, That whosoever shall say unto this
mountain, Be thou removed, and be thou cast into the sea;
and shall not doubt in his heart, but shall believe that those
things which he saith shall come to pass; he shall have
whatsoever he saith. Therefore I say unto you, what things
so ever ye desire, when ye pray, believe that ye receive them,
and ye shall have them." Dr. Charles Price's book, *The Real
Faith,* deals beautifully with this subject.

But let us make a few brief remarks. The important
thing to consider is this: many good Bible scholars feel
that verse 22 which says, "Have faith in God," should read,

"Have the faith of God," or "Have God's faith," or "Have the God kind of faith."

We are dealing with a situation much like that in James 5. Jesus had cursed a fig tree just prior to this statement. And when Christ and the disciples passed the cursed fig tree again, Peter pointed out the fact that the tree was now withered. Apparently, from what Christ says, there was a note of amazement on the part of the disciples at this miracle. Jesus then replied, and I do not believe I am overstating the truth: "Fellows, that is nothing. If you have God's faith, you can say to that mountain over there, Be thou removed, and be thou cast into the sea; and shall not doubt in his (your) heart, but shall believe that those things which he (you) saith shall come to pass; he (you) shall have whatsoever he (you) saith."

Now some people think that this saying is figurative; but I do not believe it was meant to be so. I believe Jesus pointed to a literal mountain, and promised, that if these disciples had an impartation of "God's faith," the "God kind of faith," that a literal mountain could be plucked up and thrown into the sea. It is interesting to note that the example of faith that is used in I Corinthians 13:2 is also the removal of a mountain.

In the first place, it is an impartation of God's faith. Without it you can do nothing; with it the sky is the limit. Let our faith teaching friends take note: you cannot work it up; you cannot develop it – it may only come from God. You can plead with yonder mountain until you are blue in the face; but unless God sovereignly grants you His "kind of faith," nothing will happen. If that is not an absolutely true interpretation, why have not some of them been moving any mountains lately.

Now some folk say, but if I had more faith, I could do greater things: not necessarily so. If you have the right kind of faith, you can get the job done. It is not, necessarily, the "quantity" of faith, but the "quality" of faith. Proof for this is given in Matthew 17:20. "And Jesus said unto them, Because of your unbelief: for verily I say unto you, If you have faith as a grain of mustard seed, ye shall say unto this mountain, Remove hence to yonder place; and it shall remove; and nothing shall be impossible with you."

Let us notice this passage in conjunction with the passage from Mark. The disciples had prayed for a man's son who was a lunatic. Their prayers were in vain; and Jesus, Himself, finally cast the demon out of the boy.

First, Jesus said they, the disciples, could not do it because of "unbelief." Interestingly the word "unbelief," in the original language, is a simple combination of the negative, no or not, with the word for faith or belief. "Unbelief" means, then, they did not have faith. Now, contrary to what some might say, that did not mean that they had no faith, period. The disciples had been doing some things that required faith; they simply did not have faith for this particular need.

Jesus said, if you only had faith the size of a grain of mustard seed: this was a proverbial saying for smallness. The mustard seed was said to be one of the smallest seeds in existence in Palestine at that time. What was Jesus saying? He was saying it is not the amount, the quantity; but it is the kind or quality of that faith that will remove the problem. And by the way, in this particular situation the problem was not only their lack of the right kind or quality of faith. Verse 21 says, "Howbeit this kind goeth not out by prayer and fasting." Obviously, Jesus is saying there are other elements besides faith that are involved in healings or demonic expulsions.

Back to the Marcan story: The faith necessary to move mountains is the "God kind of faith." It can only be obtained at the sovereign willing of God. Therefore, God controls it. Mere human cajoling and subsequent manipulations will not obtain or exercise this "God kind of faith." With some of the energetic, unthinking people that might start wielding that power indiscriminately, it would not be safe anywhere. We would have to spend our time ducking the mountains. Thank God, He holds on to the controls over such mighty, tremendous power.

Now God does grant miracle-working faith to certain individuals. George Mueller was granted faith for a specific purpose; and without one request for funds he supported untold numbers of orphans. When this faith is granted, as many individuals will testify, impossible tasks can be accomplished.

Some of these kinds of faith naturally overlap; the Bible does not make as plain a distinction as we seem to be making. But there is one fact I would point out to some faith teachers. God has granted some of them extraordinary amounts of faith in certain areas – I believe that. And the fallacy of some of their teaching comes at this point.

They assume that everybody can do what they are doing; and, consequently, multitudes are disappointed, simply because God has not, and probably will not, ever bring them to the lofty level of some of the faith teachers they are following.

9. Another type of faith is THE FAITH. This is simply the composite of the things that have been taught us by the Scriptures. Acts 14:22 says, "...and exhorting them to continue in the faith..."

And, we could add to this list. The Bible speaks of "little faith" in Matthew 14:31, which says, "O Thou of little faith, wherefore didst thou doubt?" Now some of our faith friends say that faith and doubt cannot be mixed; Jesus, Himself, said it could and was mixed. Read Mark 9:24, where a man said to Jesus, "Lord, I believe; help thou mine unbelief." Faith and doubt, faith and unbelief can certainly be mixed (I think they usually are). In Luke 17:5, the apostles said unto the Lord, "Increase our faith." Notice, they wanted this increase of faith to come from an outside source – namely Jesus.

Two Scripture verses say a great deal about the acquisition or receiving of faith. Romans 11:33 and 36: "O the depth of the riches both of the wisdom and knowledge of God! How unsearchable are his judgments, and his ways past finding out!" And, "For of him, and through him, and to him are all things, to whom be glory forever. Amen." Now I personally believe strongly in the free will of man. I am not a strict predestinarian whose beliefs tend toward fatalism. I have repeatedly said that man has a part in the faith transaction; God will not force His faith on anyone. And while I believe that man's free will cannot be brought into Scriptural question, at the same time, since faith proceeds on the basis of the grace of God, and God assists even our human faith, it must finally be said that faith is of God.

Thus God is the original source and fountain of all blessings. Verse 36, quoted above, tells us that no creature has any claim on God. We receive His blessings on the ground of His "mercy" and by virtue of His "grace" (His unmerited favor to us ward). And, ultimately, all we do must contribute to the final purpose of it all: "glory to God"; not the immediate needs, desires, or wants of the individual.

Romans 12:3 lets us know that in the final analysis there is nothing that we do, in this matter of faith, that should or can bring any praise to man. To God be the glory – all the glory. Should not this warn us to stay away from the man-centered, self-centered, I can do it!

One understanding of faith that would be very helpful to many people; and that would be the means of averting some of the extreme disappointments that they have when things do not always turn out the way they are believing for – is to understand that our faith is not in faith; but our faith must be in God. The same idea is helpful in the matter of prayer. Too many folk have faith in prayer, and they fail to pray with faith and belief in God.

Let us make this clearer. If a person has a very simplistic understanding of faith and believes that faith can do anything period – no ifs, buts or ands. And they believe that if they can exercise their faith, they can do anything from casting mountains into the sea, to raising the dead, to causing a million dollars to fall out of the sky, thus making them exceedingly prosperous, and all this by a simple exercise of their faith. Then, basically, we are describing a person with faith in faith.

Therefore, when they exercise their faith for a miracle, and it does not happen (which may be quite often), then they are severely disappointed (because they felt they had faith and had believed). Two options are now open to them: they may either say "I just did not have faith," or they may blame God. But the problems in both cases were that they had faith in faith.

Now if they had had faith in God, and for some reason their prayers were not answered (at least in the way they prayed them); then such a person understands that faith in God puts the burden of responsibility for an answer directly on God – I personally do not think that is unfair; but it sure makes a lot of sense. Because, after all, God has all wisdom (therefore, He knows what is best); God has all power (therefore, He could even do exceeding abundantly above all that I ask); God is an infinite Being (therefore, He knows the beginning to the end; and He knows what the consequences would be down the road if my prayer were answered the way I prayed it) – and I could go on and on.

And I simply do not understand why Bible teachers do not point these things out. Faith in faith means, in reality, my ability to manipulate God to obtain my desired end; and I am a human, a finite being, who, obviously does not always know what is best. But faith in God, means I place full and complete trust in the ability of God to know what is best and to do what is best. Praise the Lord!

I heard a seminar leader in Pennsylvania say one time, "I thank God that He did not answer every prayer I prayed." That is profound, friend. Think of young ladies who were spared a life of heartbreak when God did not permit them to have a certain young man's hand they prayed for. Think of some things in your life that you wanted so badly, but did not get. And now, looking back, you see that you also were spared from certain agony because your prayer was not answered (in the way that you prayed it).

There is another beautiful truth that is quite meaningful in helping us to understand this matter of exercising faith, and when to exercise it. In the Bible there are two basic words which are normally translated "word." These are

"*logos*" and "*rhema.*" Now it is true, for our technical
friends, that these two words overlap and are often
used interchangeably. But we shall give them distinctive
definitions.

Another instance of this kind of usage in the Bible is the
separation of man into body, soul and spirit. I, personally
am a trichotomist, that is, I believe in the separation of man
into three parts – body, soul and spirit. However, I have
pursued this study enough to know that the words for soul
and spirit oftentimes overlap; there is, in fact, no clear-cut
distinction between the two, but there is a sense in which
we can separate them.

This is true of "*logos*" and "*rhema.*" Now "*logos*" refers
back to God and to His eternal truths. Psalms 119:89 is a
good example of the "*logos,*" the Word. "Forever, O Lord, thy
word is settled in heaven." A beautiful and meaningful truth
emerges here; all that eternal Word I believe and I accept.
But all that "*logos*" is not specifically yours or mine.

For instance, when an angel appeared to Mary and
said, "Mary, you shall conceive and bear a child, and the
Holy Ghost shall overshadow you": that part of the "logos"
is not for every young lady. When God told the children
of Israel to march through the Red Sea, they obeyed and
came through unscathed. But when the Egyptians tried it,
it did not work for them. Every young lady named Mary, or
otherwise, does not have a promise to give birth to a virgin
born child: neither does every Christian have a specific
promise to walk through a sea or walk on the water.

Jesus recognized this truth. When the devil tempted
Christ on the pinnacle of the temple with the words, "The
Lord God shall bear thee up, and you will not dash your foot
against a stone," what did Jesus do? He shook His head and

said, "God's Word" ("logos") does say that; but it does not specifically say it to me at this time.

If you have never been introduced to this truth before I hope it will be meaningful. Do you remember the folk in the northern state, about whom I referred, who sat up and prayed for their deceased leader in the hopes that God would raise him from the dead. The Bible does say that if we have faith we can raise the dead; but in their case it was presumption (to take unwarranted advantage of something). As a matter of fact, presumption, in the Old Testament, is a sin. Psalm 19:13 says, "Keep back thy servant also from presumptuous sins..."

To be presumptuous is to "assume something which has no basis in fact." The devil three times threw out Scriptures to Jesus Christ: "It is written, it is written, it is written." And it was! Satan was saying, "It's in the Bible, that settles it." That, of course, is what some of our faith friends are saying; but it may turn out to be presumptuous.

Now what answer did Jesus give? He said, "Thou shalt not tempt the Lord thy God" (Matthew 4:7). What was the devil attempting to do? He was trying to test, prove, in reality, to challenge God. This specific mode of conduct was not in the best, highest interests, and God rejected a miracle.

And what was the method the devil sought to use? God's own "logos"; God's own Word! He was saying, "Now God said it, therefore, Jesus, you do it." God told one man to tell the sun to stand still; that obviously does not give you and me the right to do the same thing. There must be a balanced understanding of the Word of God.

But now let us look at the *"rhema."* *"Rhema"* also means word, but in our usage it is a particular or specific word. When God told Abraham he was going to bear a child when he was 100, and his wife was 90, that word, that *"rhema"* was only meant for this couple. That was a specific word to a specific couple. My friend, when Abraham received that Word, he believed it, had faith, and it came to pass.

If you receive a *"rhema,"* a direct Word from God, you can bank your life on it. I have known people who felt led of the Lord to claim certain things. They marched around a building, for instance, that they definitely felt that God said was going to be theirs; and they eventually got it. Other people tried the same thing and drew a blank. One had the "logos," another had a *"rhema,"* a direct Word from the Lord.

Have you not read Scripture and, one day, a Scripture which you had read many times now had special significance for you? My wife was having a pregnancy which seemed to portend a great amount of difficulty; and she, eventually, did have a number of complications. But during this time she was reading a Scripture in the Old Testament that jumped out as a specific Word of assurance that the child she would give birth to would be well and whole. And through all that difficulty, the child was well and whole, despite medical thoughts to the contrary. She received a *"rhema."* Some of the folk at the church called the child a "miracle baby" (I believe they were right). If and when *"rhema"* comes, you can strike your claim on it; it will come to pass through faith and trust on your part.

Let us look at a passage of Scripture which delineates this truth further. In Isaiah 56 we read, "For my thoughts are not your thoughts, neither are your ways my ways, saith the Lord. For as the heavens are higher than the earth, so are my ways higher than your ways, and my thoughts than your thoughts." We will stop at verses 8 and 9 before reading verses 10 and 11.

These two verses, 8 and 9, are a good indication of the "logos," the eternal Word that proceeds from God. Now a lot of faith teachers give a tremendous amount of emphasis to the Word, and, that is not a bad thing to do. After all, Romans 10:7 says, "So then faith cometh by hearing, and hearing by the word of God." But a problem can arise, as we discussed with having faith in faith, when our faith is in the Word; our faith should be in the God of the Word.

As Corrie ten Boom said, "It's not great faith in God that counts, but faith in a great God." Sometimes I pour over the Bible, and seek to understand this infinite, vast mind of the great God; and I do get a glimmer of truth here and there. But there is a means by which God can bring a portion of that infinite mind into my soul and spirit; and that is by a *"rhema."* How? Verse 10 and 11 of Isaiah 57 lets me know.

"For as the rain cometh down, and the snow from heaven, and returneth not thither, but watereth the earth, and maketh it bring for the and bud, that it may give seed to the sower, and bread to the eater. So shall my word be that goeth forth out of my mouth: it shall not return unto me void, but it shall accomplish that which I please, and it shall prosper in that thing whereto I sent it." Read the entire chapter of Isaiah 56 and see the beauty of this truth. When God drops a *"rhema,"* a specific, special Word of truth into your heart and life – watch out! You are getting ready to move things for God. But to attempt to move them without that *"rhema,"* may prove to be only presumption on your part.

...spiritual organism of Christ.
...an indivisible unit...
...in session twenty-four hours a day...

12

What is the Church?

Before we can ascertain what the "spirit of denominationalism" is, we must first arrive at an understanding of what the church really is. Many misconceptions about the meaning of the church are in vogue today. I believe one of the classic responses to certain misconceptions about the church was spoken by A. W. Tozer. He said, "One-hundred men loosely knit together in fellowship no more make a church than eleven dead men make a football team." Every kind of supposed meaning is given to the word church: from a building to a denomination. In light of such widespread, divergent views about the meaning of the word, let us look at the true biblical view of the word "church."

Let us, first, look at the meaning of the English word that is usually found in Scripture (translated from the Greek word *ecclesia*). It is often pointed out, and rightly so, that the English word "church" does not have a biblical origin. The word comes to our modern English from a Teutonic or Middle English heritage (these forms were *kirche, kerk, kirk*). These forms of the word were derived from the Greek word *kuriakos* (i.e. belonging to a lord or master) and is found in such passages as I. Corinthians 11:20 and Revelation 1:10. The Greek word *to kuriakon* was used first of all to refer to the house of the Lord, then of the people of the Lord.

In a true, basic sense, the word "church" does not (from its etymological derivation) mean the same thing as the biblical word *ecclesia* (the word usually translated into our English versions as the word "church"). This use of the word *kuriakos* (church) had its origin around 200 to 300 A.D.

Does this not, then, as some critics charge, invalidate the use of the word "church" in our discussion of its Greek counterpart *ecclesia*? We believe not. There are other non-biblical words that are used to express or translate biblical ideas or meanings (e.g. the word trinity). The problem of understanding the meaning of the word church does not arise from the mere use of the word; rather, it arises from the incorrect manner in which the word is used. Whether the word *ecclesia* is translated church, assembly, or even if some special word were formulated to express its meaning, the same problem of understanding what it means might arise.

No, the word church is a suitable word to be used in translating the word *ecclesia.* The matter of vital concern is: what is the meaning of the original word *ecclesia*? And how is the word *ecclesia* used in the New Testament? To arrive at an answer to these two questions is to understand what the church really is (in a biblical context). **Therefore, we shall use the words *church* and *ecclesia* interchangeably in our discussion.**

The word *ecclesia* is derived from the words *ek,* out of, and *klesis*, a calling. In the King James Version the word "church" is used 80 times, and the plural "churches" at least 35 times. These words are always translations of the Greek word *ecclesia* (with the exception of Acts 19:37 which is properly translated in the NASB "robbers of temples"). The word simply means to call out a group of people for a particular reason, or to form an assembly for a particular purpose. A study of the word *ecclesia* in the Bible will reveal that it is not always used to convey a spiritual meaning, as we shall subsequently show.

Now let us point out the ways the word church or *ecclesia* is used in the scriptures. First, as pointed out above, there is a usage of the word in the Bible which has no intrinsic spiritual or religious meaning. For instance, Acts 19:39 says, "But if ye inquire anything concerning other matters, it shall be determined in a lawful assembly" (church or *ecclesia*). Here the word merely designates a group of Ephesians who are in uproar against the apostle Paul. And they are, in fact, called in Scripture an assembly or church (*ecclesia*). Verse 32 indicates it was a "confused" assembly (*ecclesia*), and verse 41 says that the assembly (*ecclesia*) was eventually dismissed.

Thus we have a biblical usage of the word which carries with it a non-spiritual meaning. Therefore we conclude that the word may refer to any assembly of people. The people may come together for honorable or dishonorable purposes, and the meeting may be called or assembled by impulse for whatever reason. Obviously this is not the normal manner in which we use the word church or *ecclesia*.

Secondly, it is usually pointed out that the word is used in the Septuagint (pre-Christian Jewish translation into Greek of the Old Testament) to designate a special gathering of the Israelites. This would constitute a called-out group of people for some particular purpose. This second meaning has little significance for our study.

One writer points out that he believes the word *ecclesia* should not be translated church in the earlier parts of the New Testament, because it does not bear the later, technical meaning that we usually give to the word. However, I would disagree with this assessment. For instance, I have before me a dispensational theology book. One of the primary matters for discussion is the question: When did the church begin? This is, normally, a hotly debated issue. The answer to this question is important in formulating certain theological positions. Therefore, if a group of translators were to decide, arbitrarily, when and when not to translate the word *ecclesia* as church (or by some other designated word), we would end up with a commentary on the Bible, and not a translation of the Bible. No, let the various writers (Scofield, Ryrie, Dake, et al) annotate their opinions on this matter.

Lastly, the word church or *ecclesia* has distinctively New Testament meanings. These meanings must be gleaned from the context of the various passages. And while we believe there are certain technical, discernible meanings of the word, we also believe that the Bible never attempts to be as precise and concise in conveying all its truths as human nature would like.

Therefore, in the matter of revealing truth about the church, the Lord did so in broad understandable principles; not in fixed, absolute, voluminous discussions about every minute aspect of this truth. Can we not immediately see where many of our problems arise from? From our human attempt to understand truth, we are soon led into vast volumes that result from human efforts to explain and comment on every little point that arises about such truth. Sooner or later we come to equate our thinking on such subjects as equal to the Bible (this may be either from a practical or stated position). And the end result is heated argumentation that leads to divisive results within the body of Christ. After all, such argumentation does not seem to convince our opponent of our position, as much as it tends to confirm our own opinions and harden our attitude toward our brother.

In the New Testament we have developed what we shall refer to as a technical or specialized meaning of the word *church* or *ecclesia*. This meaning carries two distinct forms. These may be referred to as the **visible** and the **invisible** churches. All of the New Testament references can be correlated with one of these two categories.

(1) The visible church may be recognized as a distinct, local group of people. Letters or statements were addressed to an assembly at a particular geographical location.

"Unto the church...which is at Corinth" (I Corinthians 1:2).

"Unto the churches of Galatia" (Galatians 1:2).

"John to the seven churches which are in Asia" (Revelation 1:4).

(2) The word *church* may be used in the sense of the group of people who compose the local assembly.

"What? Have ye not houses to eat and to drink in? Or despise ye the church of God" (I Corinthians 11:22).

"Neither doth he himself receive the brethren, and forbiddeth them that would, and casteth them out of the church" (III John. 10).

"Take heed to all the flock...to feed the church of God" (Acts 20:28).

"If therefore the whole church be come together" (I Corinthians 14:23).

(3) The word *church* or *ecclesia* is used to describe all the Christian groups and assemblies that existed in the New Testament. These groups and assemblies, that held to the basic Christian doctrines revealed by God, were, of course, distinguishable from the other groups or assemblies that existed in the world.

> "Give none offense, neither to the Jews...nor to the church of God" (I Corinthians 10:32).

> "That thou mayest know how thou oughtest to behave thyself in the church of the living God, the pillar and ground of the truth" (I Timothy 3:15).

The teaching and revelation of the church seems to take on a progressive form in the New Testament. Careful study will reveal that the New Testament begins with teaching concerning the visible, distinct form of the church, and only later on develops and reveals the spiritual, higher, true nature of the church. It is this visible form of the church that, following Apostolic days, has developed into numerous distinct groups and denominations.

Church history seems to reveal that slight or major doctrinal differences would cause a group to break away and begin a new, distinctive unit of professing Christianity. Each new group, of course, would claim a purer form of New Testament Christianity. With the proliferating number of church bodies, each claiming division for purity's sake, should not the church today be a purer form of New Testament Christianity? Obviously, something is wrong with the logic that produces this expansionistic spirit that leads to numerous other denominations and cults.

We are now brought to the highest developed form of the new Testament *ecclesia*: the "invisible" church (the true church). This is the *ecclesia* "Which is his body" (Ephesians 1:23). In this church every member has the one "Spirit of God" dwelling in them (Romans 8:9), and its members "are builded together for an habitation of God through the

Spirit" (Ephesians 2:22). Marvelously, **every** member of this church is regenerate (Ephesians 5:27), and every one of them "have access by one Spirit unto the Father" (Ephesians 2:18). And, furthermore, they all share in the "like precious faith" which was granted "through the righteousness of God and our Saviour Jesus Christ" (II Peter 1:1). The membership rolls of this church are composed only of the regenerate, Christian man and woman. All their names are "written in heaven" and they have come into an indissoluble relationship "to the general assembly and church of the first-born" (Hebrews 12:23). Does that sound like your average denominationally structured congregation?

Notice these beautiful facts about this spiritual church: Christ is the head (Ephesians 1:22), and the members are His **body** (Ephesians 1:23). Christ is the bridegroom, and they are the **bride** (Ephesians 5:25-32). Christ is the "chief cornerstone" (Ephesians 2:20), and they are "an holy temple in the Lord" (Ephesians 2:21). The relationship of Christ to this church is supreme, sovereign and is not superseded by anything or anyone else. His relationship to the individual members of that body is not conditioned on, consequent to, or conferred by, either hierarchy or humanity. Every member has direct access, through the Holy Spirit, to the Head. Praise The Lord!

The church "invisible" is, thus, the **organism**; which is to be distinguished from the church "visible" – the **organization**. Failure to distinguish between the organism and the organization of the church has led to error and frustration, and Satan has used this device to keep multitudes from coming to Christ. After all, membership in the church visible does not assure membership in the church invisible. The failure to distinguish the validity of the two spiritual entities has been two-fold in its disastrous results.

First, multitudes have been dismayed at the inconsistencies, sin, prejudice, and intolerance of some denominationally structured church organizations. Their misunderstanding about the proper distinction related above has caused them to fail to realize that many, in some cases the majority, of these "church members" are not members of the body of Christ. Second, members of a local church, for the same reason, have developed a false security about their salvation and are merely churched sinners, never having been truly born-again, and are lulled to sleep in a pious religiosity, never having known Christ. One is immediately led to see the importance of grasping the important distinction between the organism and the organization.

The most fatal result of failure to distinguish the essential difference between these two entities is the tendency for various churches and denominations to lay claim to being the only true church on earth. Such nonsensical claims lead to the grossest of errors. One wonders why such people fail to look at the historical examples and failures of those who made such claims – and the disastrous results that followed their claims. In my opinion, such a claim not only fails to recognize the simplest of Biblical teaching on the matter, but leads to the foulest, most dangerous and damaging of consequences. It is strange that any Protestant denomination would claim to be the one true church. And this is especially true since Roman Catholicism and the Greek Orthodox churches, alone, can lay any pertinent historical claim to continuity of structure for any great length of time. I believe Roman Catholicism's claim that Peter was their founding father is as fallacious as those who claim other reasons for the supremacy of their churches.

I even know people who do not subscribe to the one visible, true church concept, who fall prey to the consequences of this theory. For instance, there is the new ecumenical movement pushing for denominational mergers. And other, of a different ilk, talk of bringing the "body" together. The Bible has news for both segments of the church world: the **body** has never been divided. Scripture plainly declares "There is **one** body" (Ephesians 4:4). Brother, you cannot divide the indivisible; there is no plurality of singularity that can be mathematically restored. The true church, the body, has never been divided and can never be reunited. The sooner we stop pushing our manmade resolutions and mergers, and accept the fact that regenerate men and women are "in Christ" and are members of one body, the sooner Christ's prayer of John 17:11 will be answered.

Denominational bodies can, and perhaps in some cases should, be reunited, but the true church is an indivisible unit of blood bought men and women whose names have been written heaven. One may or may not subscribe to the view that one may be lost after salvation, but the end result of this view, in relationship to membership in the invisible church, is one and the same. The only possibility of removal is by God, from the "Lamb's book of life" (Revelation 21:27), and the church visible has no power to invoke its excommunicative process in relationship to the eternal church. One may be falsely accused, and unfairly disfellowshipped from the church visible – but only God can exercise the divine prerogative to dismiss one from the one, true church.

Let us quickly state, lest it be construed that we are totally disparaging or disavowing the visible, organized church, that this is not our purpose. There is a place for both, properly distinguished, as we shall point out later. But it must be made crystal clear that membership in any earthly institution does not guarantee membership in the true body of Christ. Neither does failure to join a church disallow membership in the body of Christ. A sense of responsibility acquired after salvation may certainly point one toward membership or relationship to a local church body, but non-membership does not delete one's relationship to the one, indivisible body of Christ.

This spiritual church knows only one leader. While extreme emphasis upon the authority of the visible church may lead to the excesses illustrated by the Roman church, proper emphasis upon the spiritual church will recognize Scriptural truth. For God, hath given Him, Christ, "to be the head over all things to the church" (Ephesians 1:22). The Hottentots, stranded in the murky jungles of Africa, whose only claim to being a Christian is the simple faith and trust he placed in Jesus through the witness of an itinerant missionary, is a member of his church and claims Christ as the head. He is the member of no recognized, earthly, institutionalized body called a church (perhaps he would not recognize the word "membership" if he heard it), but he is a member of the heavenly church of the first-born whose names are written in heaven. And as a believer in Christ he has become one of the "elect of God" (II Timothy 2:10), chosen in Him before the foundation of the earth (Ephesians 1:4). What a pointed, true example he becomes to those who claim they constitute the one and only true body of Christ on earth.

What constitutes the New Testament Church? J. C. Ryle said it better than I could ever say it: "The existence of this Church does not depend on form, ceremonies, cathedrals, churches, chapels, pulpits, fonts, vestments, organs, endowments, money, kings, governments, magistrates, or any act or favor whatsoever from the hand of man. It has often been driven into the wilderness, or into dens and caves of the earth, by those who ought to have been its friends. Its existence depends on nothing fundamentally, but the presence of Christ through the Holy Spirit; and this, being ever within it, the Church cannot die."

This spiritual church is the "mystery of Christ. Which in other ages was not made known unto the sons of men, as it is now revealed unto his holy apostles and prophets by the Spirit" (Ephesians 3:3-6). It is the "bride of Christ" (Eph. 5:25-33), soon to be raptured into His presence (I Thessalonians 4:16-18). It is the "glorious church, not having spot, or wrinkle, or any such thing but it should be holy and without blemish" (Ephesians 5:27). Membership in this church makes us become "members of His body" (Ephesians 5:30). Members of this church are also "a chosen generation, a royal priesthood, an holy nation, a peculiar people" (I Peter 2:9).

Let us insert in this section a most pertinent statement. Neither church, visible or invisible, is a church building. If men could understand the truth of this statement, they would not be nearly as inclined to place unscriptural demands upon people that relate to the place of worship. Sinners (because of their appearance or demeanor) are forbidden entrance to many church houses because of some supposed sanctity that resides in brick, mortar and wood. First, I have found no evidence whatsoever that the early church even had buildings to worship in before 200 to 300 A.D. Secondly, God does not dwell in buildings, He dwells in men (I Corinthians 3:16; John 4:23, 24).

Earthly, visible churches may become separatist, cultic, exclusive; in fact, nothing more or less than spiritual country clubs who reserve their membership for a select few. Perhaps, in fairness of judgment, they may, more unconsciously than consciously, become highly oriented toward certain segments of society. But this is **never** the case with the true, spiritual organism of Christ. It knows neither Greek nor Jew nor barbarian (Romans 1:14-16); neither "male nor female" (Galatians 3:28); but in Him we are "all in all" (Galatians 3:28). It belongs to no single organized body any more than it does to any other; but it is properly the claim of all who know Jesus Christ as their Saviour. Its doors have no doorkeepers who place any kind of demands whatsoever upon any sinner whose spiritual nature has been quickened by the Holy Spirit for repentance (Matthew. 9:13); and that door is clearly marked "Let whosoever will come" (Mark 8:34). If this church sounds like the average congregations down the street, then pardon our impertinence in preparing this exposition, we simply have not heard of that earthly organization that could lay claim to such an exalted, and noble commentary. It is simply the church that is recognized by the old theologians as the holy, catholic (universal) church.

What a contrast to the visible, denominational structure of the church. The true church is in session twenty-four hours a day; while the visible church meets on Sunday morning and night, with a few scattered meetings the remainder of the week. The visible church may be in the form of a denomination claiming a few hundred years of existence, and leaning heavily upon some founding father. But the invisible church dates back to Pentecost for its visible expression, but dates back to eternity for its conception in the mind of God, and counts Jesus Christ, the Son of God, as its founder. If I miss or fail membership requirements in any other church, my prayer is: Let me be a member of that church!

Now, lest it be construed that the aforementioned statements are meant to disallow a visible, organized body, let us proceed to delineate the biblical teaching about such a church. It is clearly a true statement that the idea of organization is not incompatible with that of an organism. In fact, an organism usually requires an organization. The soul and spirit require the visible, tangible body in order to live in this earthly environment. Just as surely, the revelation of the Son of God to mankind required the incarnation – the revelation of God through the material, man-like existence of the Son of God. Just as surely, the fullest expression and revelation of the spiritual church is usually expressed through a substantive organization usually called a church.

Furthermore, these churches (the visible organizations) usually find it necessary or profitable to form some kind of united group structures. These are usually called denominations. A denomination is, according to the dictionary, a group that "accepts or supports certain principles or systems." In a technical sense, I believe that it refers to any group that meets or comes together on the basis of some agreed upon understanding or basis. For instance, I read a sign on the front of a church which said, "We are un-denominational." The sign listed services, pastor, and even the fact they were non-Pentecostal. My assessment was, and is, there are a great number of denominational undenominational churches in this world.

In a true sense, a small Bible study group, meeting for no purpose other than the agreed upon fact that they shall meet to informally study the Bible with no preconceived notions or opinions as to what it means, has, in fact, become a denomination. That one principle of agreement *denotes* the specified purpose for which they are going to assemble. And since they are going to invoke the blessings of Christ through the Spirit upon their assembly, they are now meeting as a church (Matthew 18:20) – both the invisible church (if they are regenerate), and the visible expression of the church (since they have an avowed, spiritual reason for coning together).

It is simply invalid, from a Scriptural viewpoint, and is to reason illogically, when one says that a visible, expressed, organized group of Christian people, is not compatible with Biblical teachings. It is a natural function of human beings to come together with other people; and such people usually remain together because they have certain things in common. But let us stress this fact early in this section: when these people do come together and form a church, or fellowship or denomination, that church is not a church because of methods, or machinery, or buildings; it is a church because it has people in it – and people are what that church is all about. It is a recognized fact that too many church leaders are caught up in the preservation of church structures and not in the preservation of people.

Let me take a personal digression to state my personal understanding of the value and usefulness of denominational and church organizations. Because of a personal reassessment of my personal understanding of the meaning and position of the church, I have related the following experience on several occasions. One day I was attempting to decide the question, "What is my personal relationship to the church? And, what relationship does the church have to me?" The answer came while reading the gospels. On one occasion, Jesus was confronted by some irate Pharisees and Sadducees who had spotted his disciples plucking grain and eating it on the Sabbath. To their irate, indignant response about his disciples' violation of the Sabbath, Jesus gave the following reply: "Man is not made for the Sabbath, the Sabbath was made for man" (Mark 2:27). Note: the same kind of irate, indignant opinion is oftentimes circulated by men captivated by the "spirit of denominationalism," who also base their misconceptions on legalistically oriented opinions.

But my spirit translated Jesus' reply to these legalistic individuals into a Biblical understanding of my personal relationship to the visible church: "Man is not made for the church (the visible organization), but the church (the visible organization) was made for man." The church visible is merely a vehicle, an instrument, that may more favorably enable man to mature, worship, and function as an emissary of Christ in this dispensation. Eminent Bible scholars, such as Chafer and Schofield, declare that the church has no responsibility upon it; all responsibility is upon the individual.

Traditionally, the kinds of church government have taken three major forms. We shall not deal with these extensively, however, a basic understanding of them is helpful in grasping certain elements of our study. First, there are churches adhering to the "Episcopal" form of government. This form of government operates with supreme authority invested in a bishop (Greek *episcopos*, bishop or overseer). Usually the laity have little or no voice in this system of church government. Many Bible scholars feel there is no Scriptural justification for this form of church government (Ryrie, Bruce, Morris, et al).

Second, there is the so-called "Presbyterian" form of church government. It utilizes a group of presbyters who form the Presbytery. These are elected by the membership. This form of church government is somewhat similar to the government in the United States with elected representatives serving in various levels of authority. Interestingly those who hold to the Episcopal form of church government usually feel it is the one and only pure form, while those holding to Presbyterianism do not usually hold that it is the only form of polity in the New Testament.

Third, there is a form called "Congregationalism." As the name implies, the emphasis or stress is on the place of the congregation in the church. Each congregation is equal in this system, and no superior organization, or associational office can intervene or separate the local church from its direct responsibility and answerability to the Head of the church, namely Christ. The principal arguments of this philosophy are based on the fact that Christ is the Head of His church (Colossians 1:18), and that there is a priesthood of believers (I Peter 2:9).

In order to conclude this area of study let us look at the tree chief classes of men who may be considered officials of the local church: namely, bishops (overseers), presbyters (elders), and deacons (servants). It is generally agreed that the bishop and elder are one and the same office, and we concur. For instance, in Acts 20:17 Paul summons the presbyters of Ephesus to come and meet him, and, upon their arrival, he calls them bishops (Acts 20:28). Other scriptures apparently supporting this view are: Philippians 1:1; I Timothy 3 in connection with I Timothy 5:17-19; Titus 1:5-7. This generally drawn conclusion is that elder denotes rank of office; bishop the duties of the office. The deacons probably busied themselves with the material and financial aspects of the church's program.

My study has gleaned several facts which are worthy of mention, but which space will not permit the development of. The apostolic office is no longer apropos to this generation. While I personally believe the apostolic function is in vogue (Ephesians 4:11), the office ceased with the death of James. Only the apostle Paul had a special calling in apostolic office function (I Corinthians 4:21; II Corinthians 10:8). Further, there is no instance in the church where one church dictated to another church or intervened in its affairs. A careful study of Acts 15 will reveal that this council was no exception to this rule. There is no example of more than one church in one given locality. And, further, the only membership mentioned in the Bible is membership in the Body of Christ (which we have declared to be the invisible church). And most Bible scholars are agreed that the Bible knows no basic distinction between the laity and the ministry (as the term is used today, and, we may add, incorrectly).

Certain conclusions are readily drawn. It has been pointed out by other writers that no large Protestant body lays claim in any official document to having divine right for its form of church government. Further, most denominational forms are not totally incorporated within one of the three major systems discussed (Episcopalian,

Presbyterian, or Congregational). They are usually an admixture of these. Some church historians have noticed a gravitation of the three forms toward similar methods of life and work.

The form of the church (visible) does not seem, therefore, to be of supreme importance since Scripture is not precise in defining its organization. As long as it does not violate scriptural truth and individual liberties, the Lord may certainly bless and anoint it. This would depend, or course, upon its continued conformity to God's will. An Anglican Bishop is quoted as saying, "Christ left the Church to organize its own form and order." The sensible, logical position is that if a particular form of church government has been developed by the leading of the Lord, and has proven helpful in carrying out the stated functions of the church: such as evangelism, education, worship, nurture etc., it may claim to be God's will.

Since some form of all three major types of church government are said to be supported by Scripture; and since this is obviously true from a practical standpoint, evidenced by the fact that many denominations claim to be organized by one of the three forms of church government; and since Scripture is not nearly as precise in delineating the forms of church government as men: it appears, therefore, that absolute support for any particular form is hard to come by.

The evidence that no denomination has right to claim divine infallibility (or anything approaching this) for its governmental form is evidenced by the legal procedures of the various churches that permit changes in its structure. Church polity, for instance, is codified, then modified, and sometimes rescinded. In face of the facts, what person or persons can, with a straight face, lay any such claim as divine function to its organization – and if so, what is the difference from claiming that it is the "one true church?" Obviously none! But the one true church is, as we have pointed out, an indivisible unit. Let us use this foundational study of what the church is to serve to undergird our look at the "spirit of denominationalism."

An old Hebrew prayer puts it well:

"From the cowardice that shrinks from new truth,
From the laziness that is content with half-truths,
From the arrogance that thinks it knows all truth,
Oh, God of Truth, deliver us."

About the Author

Philemon G. Roberts, MDiv, DMin resides in Lakeland, Florida and has been intimately associated with the faith-based movement as a pastor and denominational leader. He served with the United States Air Force during the Korean War and then began his quest for higher education earning degrees at Lee College, Florida Southern College, Emory University (Candler School of Theology), and Luther Rice Seminary (DMin). Phil was selected as an Outstanding Man in Religion and served in the unique capacity as Chaplain for the Tampa Showman's Association.

Dr. Roberts served twelve years on the Board of Trustees of Lee University and was a founding member of the Board of Regents of Oxford Graduate School serving that institution for twenty-five (25) years. His interest in higher education and a keen sense of Biblical Theology has produced quality written and spoken material. *Absolutely Sixteen Feet* is a collection of twelve (12) of his sermons.

www.ingramcontent.com/pod-product-compliance
Lightning Source LLC
Chambersburg PA
CBHW021102090426
42738CB00006B/470